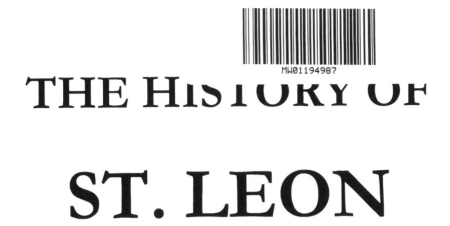

THE HISTORY OF

ST. LEON

(1781-1967)

by

Dr. Cletus R. Bulach

Vabella Publishing
P.O. Box 1052
Carrollton, Georgia 30112
www.vabella.com

Manufactured in the United States of America

Library of Congress Control Number: 2013922449

13-digit ISBN 978-1-938230-64-6

10 9 8 7 6 5 4 3 2 1

Acknowledgments

Were it not for officials at Xavier University, this book would never have been written. As part of the Master's Degree, a student had to do a research project. I chose to write the History of St. Leon as my research project. Gene McCann, who was the editor of the Lawrenceburg Register at that time, told me he would pay me for the rights to publish it when it was finished. I agreed and Gene and I took many pictures of structures in St. Leon that were still standing at that time. Many of those pictures are included in this revised version of the History of St. Leon.

There were many other individuals who were of great assistance in writing this book. Father Lawrence Frey, who was the resident priest from 1962-1967, helped me search parish records. As I dug into the history, there were many stories about what happened in the past. The following individuals helped to verify whether the stories were factual or just rumors: Albert Schuman, Edmund Andres, my aunts Mrs. Marie Pohlman and Cornelia Bulach, My uncle Joe Bulach, my mom Bertha Kraus Bulach, Bernard McCann, William Hyland, Albert Volk, John Andres, Sister Margaret Clare, Rose Schuman, William Wuestefeld, Leonard Bischoff, Ed Frey, and John Moster.

After the 1967 version of the History of St. Leon version was written, Bernadette Stenger wrote "Through the Years in St. Joseph's Parish." She wrote a about the church history which included a lot of material from what I wrote in 1967 version. Joyce Baer, Genealogy Specialist at the Lawrenceburg Public Library has also been very helpful. Her power point presentation on St. Leon has a lot of historical information.

Last, but not least, I want to acknowledge the sacrifices my family had to make for the many hours spent on this endeavor. The first edition took over a year to write, and the second edition, going back to St. Leon and Dearborn County getting new material for the rewrite, took another year of effort.

Dr. Cletus R. Bulach

Table of Contents

Foreword

The first version of the History of St. Leon was written for my Master's Thesis at Xavier University. This version was sold to Gene McCann, who was the editor of the Lawrenceburg Register at the time. He edited my work and had it typeset, but it was never published.

Sometime in the early 1990's, I asked if I could have the file he created on the history and if I could publish it. Gene gave me the file and permission to publish it. After many years of procrastinating, I have finally found time to do that. The revised version has all of the original material, but I have added personal anecdotes about memories as a child and teenager growing up in St. Leon. So the historical version now has a personal touch of what it was like to grow up there in the 1940's and 1960's.

Very little new material about St. Leon after 1967 has been added. St. Leon today has changed a great deal, and I did not want to spend the time and effort required to bring it up to date.

The history was written for the benefit of anyone who is interested in how a town such as St. Leon developed from nothing to the town is was before the development of the freeways. It begins with a point outside of St. Leon and gradually narrows the scope until what happened in St. Leon is the focus. A brief description of Dearborn County and Kelso Township are the background. Following this, explanations are given for the early settlement; the early land owners; their means of livelihood; the educational, and the military, political, and church history. The system of town government and some of the decisions made are examined. Throughout the history an attempt was made to show how life in the late 1800's and early to mid-1900 differs a great deal from life today.

Pictures of the church were chosen for the front and back cover of the book because of its importance for the development of St. Leon. Were it not for St. Joseph's Catholic Church, St. Leon might have been entirely different. In its heyday in the late 1800's and early 1900's, St. Leon was a very prosperous community with its mills, grocery stores, distilleries, taverns, and other stores and shops. At that time transportation was limited to travel by horse and wagon. With the coming of railroads, the automobile, electricity, and roads/highways, change came that was inevitable. I have tried to describe how this change came about. Some of the pictures in this book were taken in 2013 because the ones taken in 1967 have been lost.

Chapter I

Background

It was a summer day in August of 1781. A group of approximately 100 Revolutionary War soldiers were traveling by boat down the Ohio River. They were travel weary, poorly supplied, and hungry. They decided to set up camp on the right shore at the mouth of a large creek about 10 miles below the Great Miami River. As they set up camp and prepared to eat, they were suddenly attacked by a large band of Indians. The soldiers fought heroically while their ammunition lasted, and when this was gone they got in their boats and tried to escape down the river. They were not successful in escaping and were captured.

It was on this 25th day of August 1781 that the history of Dearborn County[1] and St. Leon began. This minor episode of the Revolutionary War went down in history as Lochry's defeat. Colonel Lochry was the leader of these soldiers. They were to rendezvous with Colonel George Rogers Clark farther down the river and help him fight the Indians who at that time were fighting for the British. Unfortunately, they were ambushed and captured before they met with Colonel Clark. Approximately 40 of the soldiers were killed, and the remainder was taken prisoner to Detroit, Michigan[2].

This event was important for Dearborn County and St. Leon for three reasons: 1) it was the first event of major importance in this territory; 2) the place of ambush was named Lochry's Creek after the leader of the expedition. This creek forms the southern boundary of

Dearborn County and is called Laughery's Creek today;[3] 3) When the war was over, some of these men returned and settled in the St. Leon and Dearborn County area. They remembered the beautiful country they had passed through on their way to and from Detroit. Two examples of this occurrence are George Mason and Valentine Lawrence. These two men were soldiers in Colonel Lochry's force. Both men returned to Dearborn County and settled in the St. Leon area. These two men will be further discussed in the next chapter[4].

During the Revolutionary War and until 1790, the area consisting of Dearborn County and St. Leon was part of Virginia. One often hears the people of this area refer to people from Virginia as hillbillies. Now that everyone knows that this land was part of Virginia and that indirectly, they are also hillbillies, maybe they will find another name for people south of Indiana that has a different connotation.

After 1790, boundaries changed every few years. At different times, the present Dearborn County was part of three different counties. These counties were Knox County, Indiana, Clark County, Indiana, and Hamilton County, Ohio. During the years of 1790-98 this area was part of Knox County. It was during this period that General Anthony Wayne fought the Battle of Fallen Timbers against the Indians. After this battle he secured a treaty with the Indians which established the Greenville Treaty Line in 1795. According to the treaty, settlers east of the line would not be harmed. This treaty was kept until 1811, when during the War of 1812, Indians again began harassing and killing white settlers in this area.

The treaty line extended north and south from the Kentucky River through the town of Brookville (approximately) to Fort Recovery in Ohio. Today this treaty line marks the boundary between Dearborn and Ripley Counties[5]. All land east of this line was surveyed prior to 1801, and in that year this land was part of the first public sale of lands ever made in the US[6]. From 1798-1802, this land was part of Hamilton County, Ohio and the land office for sales was in Cincinnati. The first public sale of land was through the Cincinnati Land Office[7]. Residents of St. Leon can state with some pride that the lands which comprise St. Leon and the surrounding area were part of that public sale.

After 1802 and for a period of a few months, this land was a part of Clark County, Indiana. With the increase in land sales and population, William Henry Harrison created a new county. This new county was named after Major General Henry Dearborn. At that time he was the Secretary of War under President Jefferson. Dearborn County officially came into existence on March 7th, 1803[8].

The following are some of the more important dates for those who are interested in the history of Dearborn County:

The first settlement was made in 1796 three and one half miles north of present Lawrenceburg. It was made by George Graves and Thomas Miller and their families[9].

Joseph Hayes bought 386 acres in Section 36 Township 6 North Range 1 West in 1801.

John Brown also bought land in 1801. He bought 320 acres in Section 27 Township 4 North Range 1 West[10].

As our point of focus narrows, the next logical point is the township in which St. Leon is located. It may be of some interest to know that the division of land called "township" originated in England and was first used in the New England states during the 17th and 18th centuries. It proved a very satisfactory system of dividing territory and for this reason it was used to divide what was then known as the western lands.

Kelso was the name given to the township where St. Leon is located. It was named after John Kelso, an Irishman who settled near Dover in 1813. It is of interest to note that St. Leon also had a settler by that name. His name was Seth Kelso, and he settled on the southeast quarter of section 5 in 1819[11]. Whether these men were related or not is unknown.

Kelso Township was one of the original townships formed in Dearborn County. It originally included Jackson and parts of Manchester and York townships. It wasn't until 1841 that it was reduced to its present size[12].

References

1 Atlas of Indiana, 1875 (p.8)
2 History of Dearborn and Ohio Counties, 1885 (p.74)
3 Ibid. (p.74)
4 Ibid. (p.111)
5 Fette, A. (1951). History of New Alsace, (p.8)
6 Yearbook of the Society of Indiana Pioneers, 1931 (p.12)
7 History of Dearborn and Ohio Counties, 1885 (p.111)
8 Fette, A. (1951). History of New Alsace, (p.7)
9 Yearbook of the Society of Indiana Pioneers, 1948 (p.5)
10 Atlas of Indiana, 1875 (p.7)
11 Waters, Margaret R. Indiana Land Entries, Vincennes District 1807-1877 Vol. 2, (p. 55)
12 History of Dearborn and Ohio Counties, 1885 (p.577)

Chapter II

Settlement

The above provides the background for the history of St. Leon and now we can focus more on the origins of St. Leon. Three questions come to mind when one considers the origins of St. Leon:

- How and why did the area of St. Leon come to be settled?
- What prompted early settlers to locate St. Leon at its present location?
- What kind of people were the early settlers?

To understand the answer to the first question one has to visualize the topography of the land. To the east lies the Whitewater River. To the west lies the east fork of Tanner's Creek.

A strip of land approximately nine miles wide lies between these two water courses. It is a well-established fact that early settlements tend to occur on water courses. The first settlements extended up the Whitewater River and Tanners Creek with a gradual convergence on the land lying between these two valleys. Settlements were made in 1800 and 1801 on these two water courses with the first land being bought and settled in the St. Leon area in 1815.

Another factor which caused an even settlement of this area and created the town of St Leon is Logan Creek. Logan Creek is a tributary of the Whitewater River. Early settlers came up this creek and settled along its banks. Evidence of the old road that early settlers used to go to

Harrison and Cincinnati can still be found on the east side of Logan Creek. St. Leon is the source of Logan Creek. The Jerry Bulach family farm has three creeks which feed into this creek.

The referral to an even settlement of this area in the last paragraph means that settlement of this area started in the eastern part about the same time as the western part causing an even settlement of the area. For example, the Lawrence families came up the east fork of Tanners Creek in 1817 and bought 1000 acres of land. Some of this land was in Sections 1, 2,10,11,12, and 15[1]. At that time, they owned the land where the present town of St. Leon is located. Many of the other settlers came up Logan Creek and purchased land about the same time. Some of the Lawrence settlers went west and settled near the present town of Lawrenceville. Supposedly, that is the reason for the name of the town, but I was unable to verify that.

There is still another reason for the settlement of this upland area. Looking at the area today, one might wonder why anyone would want to settle these thin clay soils and rocky slopes when bottomland along the river was available. The early settlers considered this land to be better than the river bottomlands. It was well drained and had an abundance of springs. Also, decayed forest materials had added a coat of humus to soil making it very fertile.

The woods also supplied game and forage for stock. The small valleys had more than enough acreage for hand cultivation. The uplands were freer of mosquitoes and the water was purer than in the bottom areas. Travel in these upland areas, in spite of the roughness of the territory, was easier than in the low marshy areas[2]. Consequently, St. Leon was settled because it lay between the Whitewater River and Tanners Creek and because Logan Creek made it easily accessible to a more desirable upland area. These are the reasons why the St. Leon area was settled, but does not explain why the town is at its present location.

Most towns are located at a crossroad and this true of St. Leon, Dover, and New Alsace. Why the roads tend to cross at a certain place is another story. Could they have crossed 1000 yards further north or south? The answer is no because of the survey lines that were laid out before the town was settled. Roads have a tendency to follow section lines. A check of the map of Kelso Township shows that the road running east and west follows the section line separating Sections 1 to 4 and Sections 9 to 12. In the early days, almost all roads followed section lines because people bought land by section number or parcels within sections.

A town developed at the crossroads because this location was where the four sections of land came together. A section of land consists of 640 acres. A purchase of a quarter of a section was 160 acres. During the early sale of land, people tended to buy a quarter section of land, and they usually located their house in one corner of the quarter section. The corner chosen was usually that corner nearest the road and nearest the closest neighbor. This resulted in four houses being built where these four quarter sections of land met and where the roads crossed. With four houses in close proximity a small village was formed. Eventually, an inn or tavern for travelers was opened, then a store, and as the village grew, other businesses.

To summarize, because roads tend to follow section lines, a crossroads developed at this spot. The merging of the four quarter sections of land enabled early landowners to build their homes in close proximity at the crossroads for security and convenience. This location was easily accessible from four directions, had small stores and catered to travelers. As more houses were built this place continued to grow and eventually became St. Leon. How this place got its name will be presented in Chapter 5.

Early Settlers

The early settlers/landowners of St. Leon can be classified into three types. These three types are: the hunter, the hunter/farmer, and the permanent settler[1]. The first type, the hunter, usually had a small garden and the barest essentials. They were expert with the rifle and knife and were usually at odds with the Indians. The hunter was a settler who seldom bought land because, if the hunting became poor, he would have to move to another location[2]. St. Leon probably had settlers of this type shortly after 1800. It has been said that a settler of this type did come to this area in the year 1804. His name was George Mason. He eventually did buy land in 1819.

The source for the information about George Mason as a hunter settler was made by a relative in a letter to a former school teacher at St. Leon. His name was Bill Hyland. In the letter she wrote that George had settled northeast of Tanners Creek and that enroute to this place he had described his trip. It was described as a long and lonely one with no houses being seen on the east fork of Tanners Creek. I was unable to verify the name of the relative or see a copy of the letter. At the time of this writing, Mr. Hyland was very old and recalled this information from memory. We had a long discussion about his teaching in a one room school down the road from the current East Central High School. This will be further described in Chapter 6.

Although there is no definitive proof that he was an early hunter settler, there is a logical explanation that it could have happened. First, he was a member of Colonel Lochry's force during the Revolutionary War. He was one of the prisoners who were taken to Detroit[3] and put in prison by the British. When he was released, many of them walked back to their families/home. They made several trips through the area later known as Kelso Township, once as a prisoner and once as a free man returning home. The Revolutionary War ended in 1783. We have no idea what he did until the 1804, but supposedly he was back in the area in the early 1800's. He may have come to like this area. He definitely was good with a gun or he would not have been a soldier. He also was listed as a soldier of Dearborn County in the War of 1812.

There are also two other Masons listed as soldiers of Dearborn County in the War of 1812. They are Philip and Daniel[4]. It is thought that these men are George Mason's sons. If this is true, then there is little doubt that George Mason was in this area in the early 1800's. We also know that he bought land in 1819[5]. Based on the above information; I will classify him as the first type of settler who was a hunter and did not buy land. That is why we have no official record of him until the War of 1812 and the land purchase in 1819. There are certain to be many others of this type in the early settlement of this area, but we have no knowledge of who they were?

Valentine Lawrence was also another settler of this type. He was a member of Colonel Lochry's Expedition[6] and was a Dearborn County soldier in the War of 1812[7]. He was captured in 1781 and released in 1783. We have no idea what he did in the intervening years between 1783 and 1812. He could have returned to the area as a hunter settler? He did buy land in 1817. He was also very influential in causing many other members of his family to buy land in this area.

In 1817, seven Lawrence family members migrated from Pennsylvania to this area. The heads of these families were Isaac, James, Abraham, Daniel, David, John, and Valentine[8]. With the purchase of land, the Lawrence families became the second type of settler: the hunter/ farmer settler.

Hunter/Farmer Settlers

The hunter/farmer settlers owned their own land and possessed more of the essentials for a civilized life. They were a transition class[2]. All of the early land owners of St. Leon probably fell into this category. Usually, these settlers came from the east and south and tended to have an English or Anglo Saxon heritage. Within one generation, however, almost all the lands of

St. Leon had changed hands, and the original owners had moved farther west to new lands[8].

The next type of settler was the permanent settler and they usually came from western Pennsylvania, Ohio, Kentucky, and Tennessee[9]. They probably consisted of Germans and Irish who worked in these states in order to obtain enough money to buy their own farms. As soon as they had the needed money, they bought their farm further west in Indiana.

Exceptions to this rule were the Irish and Germans who had money and immigrated to this area straight from Europe. The majority of these people migrated between 1830 and 1870. Several examples would be Joseph Bulach who came here in 1857. He eventually bought a farm from Michael Newman in 1870. He paid $5400.00 for 108 acres located in the NW quarter of Section 11. This farm is currently owned by my brother Jerry Bulach. Joe Bulach's nephew Hieronymus Bulach came in 1875 and bought a farm just west of Tanners Creek. The Joe Bulach families in Lawrenceville are descendants of this man.

References

1 History of Dearborn County, 1915, (p.175-180)
2 Burley, Carlyle. The Old Northwest, (p.26)
3 Ibid. (p. 28)
4 Ibid. (p. 28)
5 O'Byrne, Roscoe C. Soldiers and Patriots of the American Revolution, (p.288)
6 History of Dearborn and Ohio Counties, 1885 (p.201)
7 Ibid. (p. 578)
8 O'Byrne, Roscoe, Soldiers and Patriots of the American Revolution, (p.230)
9 History of Dearborn and Ohio Counties, 1885 (p.201)

Chapter III

Early Landowners

In the second chapter, the settlement of St. Leon and the types of settlers were presented. This chapter will be devoted to the listing of these early settlers and landowners. We will also provide an explanation of why St. Leon's population, prior to the arrival of the interstate system, was predominantly from a part of Germany south of Stuttgart.

The Hunters

The first settlers or hunters of St. Leon are unknown. One can only guess as to who they were. By comparing the names of those soldiers who served in the Revolutionary War and the War of 1812 with the early landowners, we can identify a few of them. For example, George Mason and Valentine Lawrence were in the Revolutionary War. They, along with Philip Mason, Daniel Mason, and William Lake also served in the War of 1812. All of these men later bought land in the St. Leon area. We can surmise that they were familiar with this area before they bought the land. It is likely that they were some of the early hunters of this area. It is quite possible the Valentine Lawrence and his brother-in-law George Mason received the land as a grant. The US government was unable to pay the soldiers of the Revolutionary War so they gave them land grants in the

Western Frontier which included Indiana, Ohio, Kentucky, and Illinois.

The Early Landowners

The next settlers were much more numerous. They are the early landowners. They bought most of the land in the Kelso Township and St. Leon area over a period of 15-20 years. Kelso Township is divided into numbered sections. Each of these sections may be subdivided into halves, quarters, half quarters, or even smaller units. (See Figure 1 of owners in 1860) If you look at Section 11, you can see the road going through St. Leon and the sharp turn in Section 2. You can also see Tanners Creek on the left and Logan Creek on the right just below the St. Leon intersection. You can also see New Alsace and Dover. Michael Newman and John Frey and John Volk owned much of the land near the town center of St. Leon. Joseph Bulach bought the Newman farm in 1870. You can look at the changes in ownership in 1875 when you look at that plat.

The following is a list of the earlier landowners and the location of the land they bought[1]. Sections 1-5, 9-12, and 13-16 tend to be part of St. Leon. You will note that all of these landowners were part of the St. Leon area. You will see the word Rel. This is an abbreviation for "relinquished." Land is relinquished when the owner stops making payments and the land is sold to someone else or reverts back to the government.

Hallomus C. Vanhontin, NE Quarter S2, 1816, Rel W half to Obediah Ellison 1826.

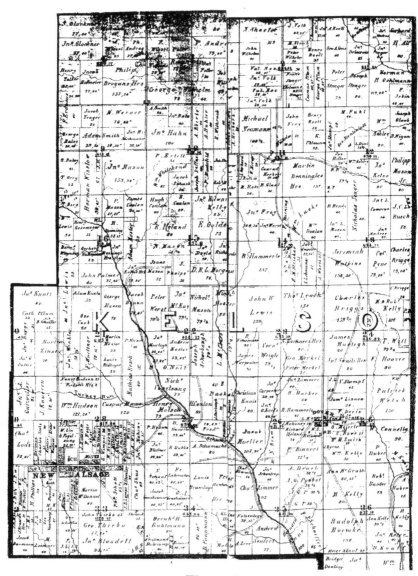

Figure 1

16

Hazekiah Coffin and Uzzia Kendall, NE half S1, 1819 Rel E half to William Hollowell.

William Douglas, NW half of S1, 1819.

Daniel Lawrence, W half of SE quarter S1, 1830.

Valentine Lawrence, SW quarter S1, 1817.

Valentine Lawrence, SE Quarter S2, 1818, Rel E half to Jacob Mason 1818.

Valentine Lawrence, SE quarter S2, 1817.

Dan Taylor, NW Quarter S3, 1820.

Robert S. Hamilton, SW Quarter S3 1819.

John Shivelay, E half S4, 6/1818.

Anthony McGinty, W half S4,1825.

Thomas Mc Clary, SW Quarter S4, 1821.

Benjamin Brown, E half NE Quarter S5, 1820.

Thomas Koates, W half of NE Quarter S5, 1820.

Seth Kelso, SE Quarter S5, 1819.

Thomas Bowman, NE Quarter S9, 1816.

Frederick Hauptman, NW Quarter S9, 9/1819, Rel to Joseph Yeager in 1830.

Philip Mason, SE Quarter S9, 1818.

James Foster, SW Quarter S9, 1818, Rel to Stephen Thom Jr.

George Lewis, NE Quarter S10, 2/1816.

William Lake, NW Quarter S10, 1816.

Robert Davidson SE half S10, 1818.

Ed Johnson & Basil Gaither, NW half S11, 1816.

Isaac Lawrence, SW half S10, 1817.

Durs Frey, NE Quarter S11, 1818.

Martin Benninger, SE Quarter S11, 1818.

Valentine Lawrence, SW Quarter S11, 1817.

William Ashley, NE Quarter S12,1818.

Daniel Mason, SE Quarter S12, 1819.

Daniel Lawrence, NW Quarter S12, 1818.
John Hall, E half, SW Quarter S12, 1824.
John Hall, W half, SW Quarter S12, 1819.
Thomas Hodge, NE Quarter S13, 1819 Rel to 1831
James Montgomery, and the W half 1832 to
Joseph Butler.
Peter Mc Keog, NW Quarter S13, 1819.
Samuel Caldwell, E half, SE Quarter S13, 1824.
Jeremiah Watkins, SW Quarter S13, 1815.
Adam Lemon, NE Quarter S14, 1818.
Henry Beamer, NW Quarter S14, 1816.
Joseph Adams, SE Quarter S14, 1816.
Nathan Blodget, SW Quarter S 14, 1818.
Isaac Lawrence, SE Quarter S15, 1824.
George Mason, SW Quarter S15, 1815.

As mentioned previously, most of these earlier landowners were Anglo Saxons with the exception of Durs Frey. To my knowledge, he is the only early landowner of German descent. In reviewing the surnames of the list above, Durs Frey and Martin Benniger are the only surnames of current residents of St. Leon at the time of this writing in the late 60's. The last male Benniger (now spelled Beneker) descendant was James, and he has passed away. He was the son of Amos Beneker who also had three daughters who married a Stenger, Bischoff, and a Knue. Their descendants still live in the St. Leon area.

Durs Frey emigrated from Switzerland. His son John C. Frey had a son John V. whose daughter was Magdalena or Lena. The Frey family descendants are still in the area. I descend from that family as my grandfather Joseph Kraus married Lena Frey. So there are also many

Bulach, Frey, and Kraus descendants from the original Durs Frey landowner.

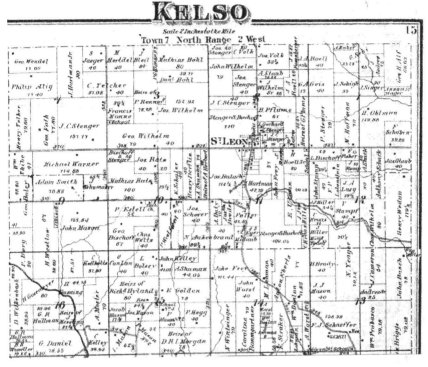

Figure 2

Permanent Settlers

Figure #2 shows landowners in Kelso Township in Sections 1-4, 9-12, and 13-16 in 1875. To find the location of the land bought by the early landowners read the abbreviations as follows: E one half, NE one fourth, S1. The east half of the northeast quarter of Section one. In figure #1, this location is the land bought by Singer and Alf in the upper right hand corner of Kelso Township.

The next landowners were more permanent and were usually Roman Catholic of German or Irish descent. In the case of St. Leon, they were of German descent. To my knowledge, all of these people came from southern Germany in an area known as Bayern. In looking at the ship records, some are listed as coming from Prussia. This was quite confusing as Prussia was an area on the south eastern shore of the Baltic Sea in northern Germany close to Poland. Further investigation revealed that this area in southern Germany was ruled at one time by Napoleon.

Napoleon Bonaparte was a French military and political leader who served as Emperor of France from 1804-1815. Through a marriage, he was somehow related to the German ruler of this area. The castle where this ruler lived is in the town of Hechingen. It is called the "Hohenzollern Castle." I visited this castle in 1993 and was told that Napoleon gave them permission to call this area "Prussia." A number of the early landowners of St. Leon come from this area of Germany. Hechingen is about 20 miles south of Stuttgart, Germany. Our ancestors (Bulach) came from a small town due east about 4 miles. That town is called Schlatt. When I visited there in 1993, I was able to talk to Bulachs who still lived there. It was interesting to find out they had no idea that there were many relatives in the US.

Reasons for German Catholic Settlement

Some of you may wonder why the population of St. Leon is chiefly Roman Catholic and from the same area of Germany. It is my opinion that the Catholic Church is partly responsible for why this happened. This opinion is based on a letter that was sent to the US Catholic Miscellany in 1828 by Father George Elder. In this letter he reported the impossibility of visiting all of the scattered Catholics in Southeastern Indiana. He proposed that the bishops of Bardstown, Cincinnati, and St. Louis should guide the migrating Catholics and concentrate them in colonies so they might not be lost to the faith.[2]

It is unknown if this practice was followed, but all indications point in favor of it. For example, Dover was an Irish community, St. Leon, New Alsace, St. Peters, Southgate, and Cedar Grove were all German communities. These German communities were further divided because each community came from a different part of Germany. New Alsace consisted of people from the Alsace Lorraine part of Germany. This area is now a part of France but in the 1800's it was part of Germany.

The citizens of St. Leon all came from an area near Stuttgart, Germany. The citizens of St. Peters, I was told, came from the northern part of Germany. The citizens of Southgate were always considered a part of the St. Leon community as they belonged to the same Catholic Church. As for the citizens of Cedar Grove, I am not sure which part of Germany they came from, but it was definitely a German settlement. The dialect spoken in these German communities tended to be slightly different, although each community could understand what was being said.

Another interesting fact is that German was the predominant language being spoken in each home until the Second World War. As a student at the University of Cincinnati, I enrolled in a class to study German. The professor was amazed that my pronunciation of the language was that of a native German. I told her that when I was a kid, I heard a lot of German being spoken. I was born in 1938 and my parents frequently spoke German. During World War II, that all changed. The citizens of St. Leon did not want to be thought of as favoring Germany over the US. Letters and communication with relatives in Germany were also stopped. All communication with our relatives in Germany had already stopped during WW I.

I distinctly remember hearing my parents and relatives speaking German when they did not want us to hear what they were saying when I was 10-12 years old. That would have been after the war was over. A frequent phrase that I heard was "Wie gehts! That was the German phrase for "How is it going!" It was not uncommon to hear this response: "The gates are alright, but the hinges are rusty!" It was a play on words from one language to the other. My brother Wes, who is several years older, still greets me with that saying and he remembers many other sayings in German.

Another factor which probably influenced people to settle where they did is the tendency for people to seek their own kind. As a result, it is quite likely that the advice of the bishops was followed. Being in the same community with a common German dialect was preferred over a community where it was different. That there is a distinct difference in dialect is based on my experience as a student who majored in German and taught it for 7 years at Western Hills High School in Cincinnati, Ohio.

I have also visited Germany, and I can definitely state that the dialect in northern Germany and southern Germany is very different. Similarly, an Irishman would rather be in an Irish community like Dover than in a German community like St. Leon or New Alsace. Keep in mind that the distance from St. Leon to Dover is only three miles. From Dover to New Alsace was only four miles.

As a person growing up in St. Leon, I learned that there were certain unwritten rules. One was that you should not date anybody from Dover. I was told that they are Irish and you need to stay away from them. There was also the advice about the citizens of Bright. They were Protestant, and we were also to stay away from them. We also had a community called Chaplow Ridge. This was an area just south of Southgate. They were called "Holy Rollers."

I still don't know what that means, but I rode my bicycle over there one day to see why I should not be over there, and I did not see anything to worry about. Growing up in St. Leon was a very interesting experience and one that no one today will ever experience. Prior to the 60's and the advent of the interstate system, everybody was Catholic, German, and a Democrat.

References

1. Waters, Margaret. R. *Indiana Land Entries,* Vol.I pp.54-55.
2. Fette, A. (1951). *History of New Alsace.* P. 72.

Chapter IV

Livelihood

In this chapter I will present how the citizens of early St. Leon made a living. I will also share what most citizens did for a living in the years prior to 1960. The early population of St. Leon consisted of farmers and various businesses to support the farm population, e.g., saw mills, mills, cooperage, cider press, tavern, etc... The farmers cleared small plots of land for gardens and small fields of grain. Their gardens provided vegetables and the grain was used to feed the animals and for grinding at the mill. Of the grains, corn was grown by everyone. Much of St. Leon is hill country, and corn left the soil exposed and subject to erosion. This land was fertile when it was freshly cleared, but continued erosion and leaching of soil nutrients caused poor soil condition.[1]

When one plot of ground was exhausted, they cleared a new one. In this way, they eked out an existence. New agricultural techniques and fertilizer have helped to revitalize the farms in St. Leon. Consequently, there are many excellent farms in the St. Leon community today. Farming today, however is very different from the way it was prior to the 1960's.

Early Farmers, Mills, and Other Support Businesses

The early farmers of St. Leon were not self-sufficient. As a result, mills and other support businesses were established. Two flour mills were established within a short distance of the St. Leon community. One mill, the Hinkston mill, was established on the Whitewater River at the mouth of Logan Creek. The other mill was the Lawrence mill on Tanners Creek shortly after their settlement in that area around 1817. It was probably located near the present State Highway #46. The farmers of St. Leon probably used these mills until John C. Stenger built a flour mill within the city limits in 1854.[2]

After 1850, several creameries were established in Dearborn County. Many of the farmers took advantage of this by raising dairy cattle and selling milk and cream to the creameries. That practice continued into the 1950's and gradually declined until there are very few dairy farms in the St. Leon area today. I remember only too well getting up in the early hours of the morning to go down to the barn and milking 8-10 cows. Twelve hours later we had to repeat the process each afternoon. If there was one thing I hated more than anything else, it was going to the barn and milking those cows. Ugh!

Getting hit in the head by one of the cows' tails did happen. Often the tail was not very clean and when we went to school we sometimes had a peculiar odor, but then so did a lot of the other kids. It was a routine for all of us that we took only one bath a week. The routine went something like this in the summer: A large galvanized wash tub would be placed on the sidewalk and filled with water. The sun would warm the water and the youngest took the first bath. There were seven children in our family and as the 2nd oldest, I was next to last. It was important to take a bath, and how clean the water was did not seem that important. My poor older brother Wes!

Many of the farmers needed utensils and other manufactured items to operate their households and farms. The selling of milk and cream was one way to get some cash for that purpose. They also sold grain, chickens, eggs, hogs, cattle, and potatoes. There were meat packing houses in Aurora and Lawrenceburg and later in Cincinnati. Hogs, cattle and chickens were sent to these packing houses.[1]

I remember, when I was a kid, that dad and other farmers would take what they had to sell to the general store in St. Leon on Monday mornings. It was operated by Joseph Schuman at that time. He would take all the produce and other things to Cincinnati and sell them. On Monday evenings, the tavern would be very busy as farmers came back to town to get their money.

In the early days and up until the 50's, practically every farm in the St. Leon area had an orchard and a vineyard.[1] Pears, apples, peaches, cherries, prunes, plums, apricots, and grapes could be found on most farms. Jellies, preserves, wines, brandies, and forms of whiskey were made from these fruits. At one time, St. Leon had two distilleries, a winery, and two cider presses.

The selling of fruit to the distilleries and the winery was extra income for some farmers. When the distilleries and winery closed, the importance of the orchards declined. This was followed by better transportation and refrigeration causing fruit to be bought more cheaply. Less and less emphasis was placed on an orchard because there was no need for them. Today only remnants of once fine orchards exist, and on many farms even the remnants are long gone. I remember the orchards of Joseph Kraus and John Andres. Picking a wagon full of apples to take to the cider press was a festive event. While the apples were being pressed to make the cider, the farmers would gather around and swap stories.

Prior to 1950, most farmers tilled and planted their own crops. It was a common practice for five to six farmers to get together and help with the planting and harvesting of the crops. The threshing of wheat and shredding of corn was often done as a group. The occasion was often festive with everybody together with their wagons and horses. The men would be out in the fields working and the women would by home cooking the noon dinner. One example would be John Andres who along with a number of other farmers owned a threshing machine that was used to harvest the wheat.

This threshing machine looked like a pre-historic behemoth beast. There was the mouth part or tray where the bundles of wheat would be carried into the body of this huge machine and the wheat and straw would be separated. The wheat would come down one chute into a sack and the straw would go out a large cylindrical chute and get blown onto a straw stack. I want the reader to visualize how this looked in a typical farmyard.

Imagine a tractor sitting about 20 feet from this huge machine. There is a belt that is hooked to a pulley or power take off on the tractor and the belt is hooked to the threshing machine. The power to operate the threshing machine is from the pulley on the tractor. When all of this is in operation, there is a low rumble. The wagons and horses drive alongside the beast and toss the bundles of wheat into this large mouth or trough. A series of chains and wooden slats carries the bundle inside the beast and knives chew it up and the wheat gets separated from the straw. The straw goes into the blower part of the beast and gets blown out onto the straw stack. The small kernels of wheat go into another part and are put in a sack. These sacks of wheat were carried to a granary and emptied for storage. When the price was right or the farmer needed some money the wheat was sold.

When I was about 12 years old, I was given the task of controlling how the straw was blown out the chute. It was every kid's dream to have that honor. Imagine sitting on top of this huge machine that was vibrating and rumbling below you. What a feeling that was! I had the rope in my hands that controlled this huge 30 foot tube that went out from the machine to the straw stack. On the end of the tube was a flap that was moved up and down depending on whether you wanted to blow straw near or far.

This allowed a person to control where the straw was going, move it up or down, and around. As the straw was blown onto the stack, another person formed the stack. It was a two person operation. The person on the machine blew it to the spot where it was needed on the stack. Once the stack was about finished, the person operating the blower had to put a cap on the stack. The cap was important because if it was not done properly, the rain would soak into the interior of the stack and it would rot. If it was a perfect dome, the water would run off and the straw stack would be dry for years.

The straw stack was somewhat of an engineering phenomenon. How could you preserve wheat straw so it was usable for bedding in the barns for more than a year? The answer was the straw stack. It had to be constructed in a location that would not get groundwater (the base) and it had to be designed so it would not fall over. It also had to be designed so the rain water would run off and not soak or rot what was inside it. That meant that it had to be fairly cylindrical and there had to be a cap that protected the entire stack.

Today of course there are no more straw stacks. Think of how the harvesting of wheat has progressed. The old process was the cutting of wheat with a scythe and beating it to separate the wheat from the straw. It took many workers to cut a few acres. Along came the binder and the threshing machine. One person could cut the wheat and put it into bundles and do 20 acres in a day. The bundles would be put into a shock and this took 2-3 workers. The shocks preserved the wheat until it became time to put it on wagons and carry it to the threshing machine for harvest.

The threshing machine and binders made the old process of cutting with a scythe obsolete. The next invention was the combine and baler and this replaced the threshing machine and straw stack. While it took ten or more people and many wagons to thresh the wheat in those days, today it takes one combine, one baler, one or two people, and goodbye to straw stacks.

With the advance of larger equipment, some farmers began farming their neighbor's and other people's farms. One such farmer, who is now deceased, was Robert Alig. He rented farms in the area and planted and harvested the crops. That practice continues today with some of the larger scale farmers tilling and planting over 1000 acres. One such farmer, Mark Schuman, farms the old Hyland farm, the Joe Kraus Sr. farm, and many other farms in the area. The Hyland farm is toward Dover, IN and north of the Gerald Wilgenbush farm. The Kraus farm is on Kraus Road not far from East Central High School.

The citizens of St. Leon today are virtually independent of their neighbors, while years ago the opposite of this was true. Today's citizens, with the help of modern machinery and techniques, can do all the work alone. If for some reason help is needed, they usually hire someone. Years ago and up until the late 50's, most farmers worked in groups. If something needed to be built or land needed clearing, a group of men would gather and complete the task. Money was seldom exchanged for this work because each knew they would need help someday. They knew they could count on each other when they needed help.

This way of working is sometimes called the community effort. The last vestiges of the community effort disappeared with the arrival of the combine and the disappearance of the threshing machine and corn shredders. There is no longer a need for large groups of men to get together to accomplish a task. All that remains of this outdated method of farming is memories. There are only a few of us left who still remember how enjoyable that was. There were large dinners, plenty to drink, a lot of camaraderie, a lot of teasing, tests of strength and skill. This was all part of this community effort. I recall a wrestling match at our neighbor Albert Wilhelm's house. I was probably about 10 years old and everyone had gathered around to watch me and another kid wrestle. That would be unheard of today.

Transportation

Transportation facilities play an important part in the growth of a town. A town which is strategically located along a railroad, river, or crossroads tends to grow rapidly. Unfortunately, St. Leon was not located on a river or a railroad. It is located at a crossroads but the traffic on these two roads has had little influence on the growth of the town. The only road of significance was US Route #1 going to Lawrenceburg in the south and Brookville in the north. The new Route # 1 bypassed the town and further diminished the importance of St. Leon. Many residents, however, were happy for the bypass because it reduced traffic at the crossroads.

In the 1800's, however, St. Leon was strategically located and it could take advantage of all traffic going east, west, north, and south. At that time the crossroads were the only roads going south to Lawrenceburg, north to Brookville, east to Harrison, and west to Sunman. Since that time new roads east and west, such as US #46, have been built. A railroad that runs east and west through Sunman and one that runs north and south from Harrison to Brookville have also been built.

The roads going east and west were built in this order. The road going down Logan Creek was the first to be built. This road is about a half mile south of the crossroads in St. Leon and just before the present crossroads of US #1 and #46. It was built by Frank Geis at a cost of $300.00.[3] This road gave the citizens of St. Leon a better route to Harrison and Cincinnati. It also bypassed a very large hill on the old east/west road that went through St. Leon. This large hill was located up the valley from the north fork of Logan Creek. There used to be a large hole in the creek at this juncture. When I was a kid, we used to ride our bikes to this hole and skinny dip.

The second road going east and west was highway US #46 which was built in 1936. The last road to be built was Interstate #74 which was completed in 1964. These last two roads have been both detrimental and beneficial to the growth of St. Leon. They were detrimental because the town of St. Leon was bypassed. They were beneficial because many people from the Cincinnati area found easy access to inexpensive land.

A number of subdivisions have been built in the St. Leon area since the opening of I #74. The first subdivision to be built was the Herzog subdivision. Joseph Herzog had lived in Cincinnati, and he bought the farm down the road from the East Central High School. I spent many hours in the early 60's working with him to clear some of that property. The two surveyors who laid out the lots were Dennis and Wally Kraus. Herzog's two sons, Louie and Henry, who were builders in Cincinnati, also helped him create that subdivision.

Since then a number of other subdivisions have been built. The easy access to St. Leon via I #74 and the presence of North Dearborn High School have made the area very attractive for new home owners. What was once a community of farmers of German and Catholic descent is now a bedroom community for Cincinnati. The current citizens of St. Leon come from all walks of life, race, and religion.

It may be of interest to know that the railroad which now goes through Weisburg and Sunman could have gone through St. Leon. Four routes were surveyed for the railroad. One of these was from Elizabethtown through St. Leon at the same approximate location as I #74. The large hill coming out of Elizabethtown was probably the reason why the Weisburg/Sunman route was chosen.

There was also a trolley planned from Cincinnati to Indianapolis. The survey for the trolley was also the current route for I #74. The trolley line was to be built in 1913. However, there was a flood that year which caused the money for the trolley to be used to repair washed out roads and bridges. This delayed the project long enough for the automobile to outdate the trolley and it was never built.[1]

The Whitewater Valley R.R. was built in 1868 and did little to help the growth of St. Leon. Freight charges to the depot in Cedar Grove hurt the businesses in St. Leon. The mills and distilleries could not remain competitive because of these charges and overtime went out of business. St. Leon was a thriving community with many businesses, but a decline started after 1885. Today, none of these mills and distilleries exist.

During the 50's and 60's the citizens of St. Leon earned their living in a number of different ways. Farming was still an occupation for many of them, but often it was something they did after their factory job. General Motors had a plant in Hamilton, OH. General Electric had a plant in Cincinnati. Seagram's had a plant in Lawrenceburg. These were the plants where most citizens tried to get on because of the higher pay scales. Some other plants with lower pay scales were Sperry Rubber which was located between Cedar Grove and Brookville. There was a roofing company in Brookville and a box factory in Harrison. There were other factories and plants in Batesville as well with Hillenbrand and Romweber being the biggest. They later merged and became Hill-Rom. Furniture, hospital beds, and caskets were a big industry in this town.

The Sperry Rubber Plant Strike in 1960-61

An interesting story about one these plants/ factories took place at Sperry Rubber. My brother Wes helped to build this factory when he graduated from high school in 1954. When the factory opened he was one of the first hires. When I graduated from high school in 1956, I also went to work there until I joined the military in 1957. On my return from the military in 1960, there was a serious labor strike at the plant and my brother and other workers at the plant who did not go on strike were talking about how dangerous the situation was. Non-striking workers were having their cars and homes vandalized. A favorite form of vandalism was a 12 gauge deer slug through a car's radiator. Dropping nails on the driveway going to and from the plant was another favorite. This conversation took place at Schuman's tavern in St. Leon. I suggested that they should go to management and ask to have a guard force to protect them and their vehicles. My brother Wes and cousin Cliff

Bulach turned to me and said, "Yeah smart guy why don't you do that!"

Well I went to management and suggested that they put me in charge of setting up a guard force. They liked my proposal and I was hired on the spot. I hired several college students and we set up a procedure for cleaning the driveways of nails and patrolling the perimeter from 6:00 p.m. until 6:00 a.m. We all had 12 gauge pump shotguns and we would walk the roof of the plant and the perimeter to watch what the strikers were doing. There was a lot of animosity between the strikers and those that went to work. Many were related and came from the same community. During the year that I worked as a guard at the plant there were many incidents that happened on a weekly basis as the strikers tried to break the strike. I will only relate four of them although there are many more.

The first incident was when the union brought a bunch of fellow union members down from Chicago to provide support for the strikers. It was a Sunday afternoon in July, and I was walking the roof of the plant in easy view of the strikers who were gathered on the road in front of the plant. There was a lot of drinking going on, and they were becoming more and more agitated. I was the only person in the plant and there were about 50 strikers walking up and down US # 52. I was getting scared they were going to come for me. They were calling me every name in the book from "Scab" to other names far more offensive. I said some prayers because it was getting worse and worse. At about 3:00 p.m. clouds formed and before long a severe thunder and rain storm broke up the strikers. To this day, I believe that had the storm not happened they would have stormed the plant to get me.

As the strike continued into more than six months, it was rumored that they were going to bring down more people from Chicago to provide support to the strikers who were growing weary of the pro-longed strike. It was about 6:00 a.m. on a Monday morning, and I was preparing to leave to go to the University of Cincinnati, where I was a freshman student at that time. The company president asked me to go down to a parking area south of the plant to see if there were any cars with license plates from Illinois.

I had an hour to go on my shift so I took my shotgun and walked behind the building where the strikers could not see me. However, when I crossed US # 52, they saw me and yelled, screamed, and called me many obscenities. I looked at them and saw a women coming down the center of the road with an umbrella. She caught me in the middle of the road and started beating me with the umbrella. The strikers were hooting and hollering as they encouraged her. I was able to run away from her back to the safety of the plant.

One cold winter night, I had to go out and clear the driveway of nails for the 2nd shift to go home. I tucked my 22 caliber pistol in my belt and told the other guard to cover me with his shotgun. I walked out to the driveway and saw about 10 strikers around a barrel that had a fire in it so they could stay warm. Several appeared drunk, and they were yelling at me and calling me names. As I stooped over to pick up the nails, one of the strikers came up to me and put his arm around my neck and had me in a head lock. He had a piece of firewood in his hand and said, "How would you like me to bash your head in?"

I was not sure what to do, so I slowly grabbed the pistol in my waist band and planned to point it at him. One of the strikers yelled "he's got a gun!" He let me go, and I walked back to the plant and counted my blessings. Things could really have gotten out of hand. I told the other guard that if it ever happens again shoot in the air, but don't shoot them.

The last incident toward the end of the strike was the most frightening. It was a Sunday evening around midnight. I was making my rounds patrolling the plant and there was a terrific explosion outside the plant. I figured they had targeted the paint shed and there would be further explosions. I called the sheriff in Brookville and told him what had happened. He told me he was not going to come down, and that this thing was totally out of control. He said that he was not going to get in the middle of it.

I then called the state patrol and they got there around 2:00 a.m. We discovered that they had blown up the pump house which supplied water to the plant. The plant was out of commission until they had the pump house rebuilt. The strike was not successful in getting the union into the plant, but it was a very trying experience for a number of St. Leon citizens who worked there.

While many citizens of St. Leon worked in plants and factories within commuting distance of St. Leon, a new source of employment had become available. Interstate I 75 was being built through Cincinnati and many bridges were being built. Several citizens of St. Leon had become foremen on some of these jobs. Joseph and Teddy Stenger were responsible for building many of these bridges, and they hired many of their workers from St. Leon.

I was one of those hires as were a number of others in St. Leon. I worked for three summers while I was a student at the University of Cincinnati. The wages were excellent and I was able to make enough money in the summers to get my bachelor's degree in teaching. We helped build all of the bridges on I #75 through Cincinnati and northern Kentucky. The last one to be built was the one over the Ohio River. I was not part of that one, and I am not sure if any of the St. Leon workers were part of that one either?

References

1. History of Dearborn County, 1915
2. Fette, A. (1951). History of New Alsace
3. St. Leon town records

Chapter V

Origins and Businesses

Anyone reading this history has to wonder where these German immigrants came from since they were all German and Catholic. There were actually two settlements during the 1800's. One was the settlement later named St. Leon and the other was a settlement about a mile away called Schaffenburg which no longer exists. Schaffenburg was located in the area where US #46 and I-74 cross and probably on land that was the Joseph Schuman farm. This farm is now owned by Walter Schuman.

Origins

It is most likely that some of the early Germans in Schaffenburg came from a town in Germany called Aschaffenburg. This town lies 120 miles due north of Stuttgart. According to Dick Stenger, [1] his ancestor John Stenger came in 1838 from a village near Aschaffenburg and probably settled in the Schaffenburg area, although that has not been documented. He confirmed that he still has relatives who live in the Aschaffenburg area of Germany. He reported that Henry Stenger immigrated to St. Leon in 1840 and Franz in 1841. He descends from the Henry Stenger line. Leo and Harold Stenger descend from the Franz line. The other Stenger family in St. Leon, i.e., Wes, Melvin, Theodore, Jake, and Tony, also descend from the Franz line.

Most of the German immigrants of St. Leon came from another part of Germany 38 miles south of Stuttgart. In tracing the ancestry of the Bulach family, with the help of my wife Joan, we found they came from a small town called Schlatt which is several miles east of Hechingen. Hechingen is south of Stuttgart and this area of Germany was called Prussia even though the State of Prussia was close to the Polish border.

I visited this town in 1993 along with my wife Joan, who is a genealogist, to see if any Bulach relatives were still there. I had an old post card that had been sent in 1898 to my Aunt Marie Bulach Pohlman, who was my dad's (Clarence) sister. The post card was written by Agatha Bulach. When Aunt Marie passed away, the post card was found in an old trunk in the attic. My first cousin Ellen Bulach found it and gave it to me to translate since I was a German teacher at Western Hills High School in Cincinnati, OH. The post card was written in 1898 and showed a picture of an inn called "zum Lamm." Translated that means "To the Lamb." At the time this post card was written, Agatha Bulach lived at this inn and hostel.

On arriving in Schlatt, we drove to the center of town, and to our disbelief, we saw the "zum Lamm" just as it appeared on the post card. I asked the young man distributing beer, if the owner of the building was around? He said she was on the third floor. I went up and knocked on the door and an 80+ year old woman answered. I spoke to her in German and told her who I was, and she said she knew nothing about Bulachs in America. I showed her the post card and she about fainted and said "Aunt Agatha." She told me that Agatha

Bulach had never married and had lived with them at the inn. I have forgotten her name, but her last name was Killmaier. I found many other relatives in this area, and they could not believe all the relatives they had in the US.

I have included this because many of the St. Leon citizens who came in the mid to late 1800's and are of German descent, more than likely came from this area that is 20 miles north to 20 miles south of Stuttgart. I can verify this to be a fact because I visited this area and found many names similar to those I knew growing up in St. Leon. I did not find any Stenger surnames.

That raises the question about why our relatives in Germany did not know anything about us in Indiana. I assume this would be true for many other German citizens of St. Leon. Prior to WW #I and II most citizens of St. Leon spoke German. When the citizens heard that the Japanese on the west coast were being put into camps, they feared the same might happen to them.

They took two steps to make sure this did not happen. All correspondence with relatives in Germany for our family stopped before WW #I, and they switched to English as the public language just prior to WW # II. However, they continued to speak German in the privacy of their homes. My older brother Wes still knows a lot of German, and I found it an easy language to learn and became a German teacher. That was because German was often spoken at our house. I know others of my age, who grew up in St. Leon, also could speak German. Joe Weldishofer comes to mind. He was the son of Florian Weldishofer. He was my dad's first cousin. Florian's father was the brother of my grandfather's wife Lena Weldishofer Bulach.

Businesses

The businesses of St. Leon were both legal and illegal. The illegal businesses were moonshine related. From 1920 to 1933 alcohol was prohibited and this caused the illegal business of moonshining. Prohibition in the United States was a national ban on the sale, manufacture, and transportation of alcohol.[2] The ban was mandated by the Eighteenth Amendment to the Constitution. Prohibition ended with the ratification of the Twenty-first Amendment, which repealed the Eighteenth Amendment, on December 5, 1933.

There is the story about one moonshiner who had his still for making moonshine in a sinkhole. Whenever the revenuers were in the area to search, this farmer covered the sinkhole with brush. According to stories I heard growing up, this moonshiner was never caught. The St. Leon area has many sinkholes caused by a layer of limestone about 10-15 feet below the ground. If a hole occurs in the limestone, water will seep through it and eventually create a sinkhole. For example, there are three sinkholes on several fields on the family farm now owned by my brother Jerry Bulach. The farm is just west of town and can be seen on the left as you approach town on US #1. (See Figure 1)

Figure 1

There were many legal businesses in the St. Leon area. Anyone reading this will wonder how all these businesses could exist in St. Leon. The reader has to remember that the citizens of St. Leon had to make almost everything they needed. In the 1800's, transportation was by horse and buggy. Going to the store meant, they had to go to one in St. Leon. Looking back on this period in history it is absolutely amazing at the variety of businesses that existed in St. Leon at that time. For example, there were six general stores, two distilleries, one winery, two cider mills, two breweries, three ice houses, one sorghum and molasses mill, two flour mills, three saw mills, a cooperage, two brickyards, three wagon shops, three blacksmiths, a shoemaker, two cigar manufacturers, a horticulturist, and a dentist.

There were also a number of people who owned threshing and shredding machines. All of these businesses existed from the mid-1800's to approximately 1930. They did not all exist at one time but most of them were operational in 1885. This is the date marking the height of prosperity for St. Leon.[2]

The six general stores of St. Leon were all located within a mile of each other. One was located along the present S. R. #46 on the Joseph Schuman farm now owned by Walter and Mary Doll Schuman. This store which was owned by Adam Schuman served the Schaffenburg settlement. He also had a huckster route. In 1888, his son Joseph Schuman bought the store and moved it to the city limits of St. Leon. He conducted his business from the same building which was later operated by his son John Schuman. On his death in 1932, his wife Rose sold the stock, except for candies and ice cream. [2]

Figure 2

In 1934, she got the post office franchise and this building was a candy and ice cream shop and post office until 1955. I remember many days going into this store for an ice cream or a piece of candy. At that time a piece of candy only cost a penny. That building still exists in the center of town right across the road from St. Joseph's church and is now owned by Eric Stenger. (Figure 2)

Figure 4

In 1860, Joseph and Mary Schuler Bulach established a general store and tavern at the same location as the present tavern. (Figure 4) They also operated a huckster route. On his death in 1876, the store was operated by his son Joseph Bulach Jr. He sold it to Joe Wintz who had it for less than a year and sold it to Joe Hoffman. He sold it to Joseph G. Schuman in 1930. This Schuman was the brother to John Schuman who operated the other store in St. Leon. Joseph also acquired a dealer's license to sell International Harvester trucks and farm equipment. His son Lawrence operated this store and tavern for a number of years. On his death, his wife Louise ran it for a number of years. She sold it to Ray Batty who operated it for a number of years before selling it to Paul Alig.

Figure 3

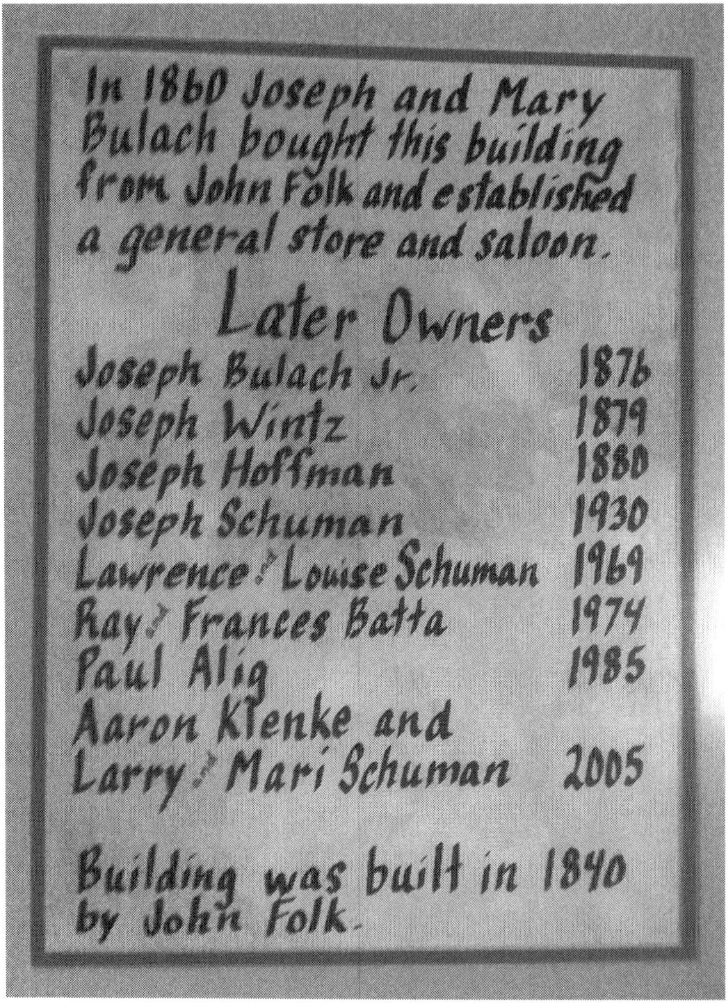

Figure 3A

He sold it to Larry and Mari Schuman and Arron Klenke in 2005. Arron is Mari's son from her first marriage. This store is now over 150 years old. It has been remodeled and added on to numerous times, but some of the original structure is still there. A distinguishing feature of the saloon is the walnut bar.

(See Figure 3) It was cut from a single tree and is the same bar built by the original owner Joseph Bulach.

There is a wooden plaque in the bar that shows who built and owned the bar up to the present time. (Figure 3A) A John Folk supposedly built the building that Joseph Bulach converted to a tavern and grocery store. In 1864, Joseph Bulach bought two acres from John Volk according to the deed records at the Dearborn County Recorders' office. He paid $1725.00 for those two acres indicating that there were some building(s) along with the purchase. That could have been his purchase of the building for the store and tavern. John Folk and Volk is the same person. In German, the letter "V" is pronounced as an English letter "F."

There were also three purchases of other land between 1863 and 1867 of adjoining pieces of property. He bought one third of an acre from Jacob Wilhelm in 1863, two and one half acres from Jacob Wilhelm in 1867, and .72 acres from Jacob Wilhelm's son Joseph in 1868. None of these purchases gave the amount of the purchase. The plaque indicates the purchase was in 1860 and that John Folk built it in 1840. This could be true, but the purchase date by Joseph Bulach is probably the 1863 date and not 1860. The date that it was built and who built it could be accurate.

A fixture at the saloon is Anna Mae Dierckman Callahan. She has been serving customers and making soups for customers for over 30 years. Her soups are a favorite for customers. My favorite is her chicken soup followed by her ham and bean soup.

Another general store was also on the crossroads in St. Leon. This store was operated by Andrew Aug in what was then called the Old Leonard House. The location of this store was located where Jake's garage was located. (Figure 5A) There were three general stores within one block of each other. Whether they were all operational at one time or not is unknown.

A fifth store was operated by a Joseph Stenger in 1865.[4] The location of that store was the first building east of town on the left side of the road. That was also the location of a winery and later a blacksmith shop that his son John H. Stenger operated. As a child of about 5-6, I was in that building when it was owned by Al Glaub. The building would have been in the same area as the parking lot for the current Family Life Center.

Figure 5A

Figure 5

A sixth store was operated by Charles Fuernstein. This store was located in the same general area as the filling station and store that was run by Irvin Fuernstein for years. (Figure 5) He sold candy and soft drinks as well. On his death, his brother Lester bought the house and his other brother Howard, called Buddy, took over the gas station. The station is currently being run by Buddy's daughter Faye and her husband Ken French.

There was another store on the square in St. Leon. It was a hardware and furniture store and was operated by Al Knecht (Figure 6). The exact history of this store is unknown, but it was later owned by Wilfred and Alfred Bischoff. The current owners of that building are Tim, Dan, and Melvin Wilhelm. At one time this was a magnificent looking building with its display windows, wrap around porch and columns. It is currently in need of renovation.

Figure 6

There were four saloons in St. Leon. Usually, they were run in conjunction with the general store. This was the case with Adam Schuman, Joseph A. Schuman, and Joseph Bulach. The exception to the rule was Andrew Aug who had a saloon near one of the flour mills. His business was composed of farmers who took their grain to the mill. While waiting for their grain to be ground, they could go to Aug's saloon to relax and have a drink. When the mill closed down in 1896, the saloon also closed.

There were two distilleries in St. Leon. One was owned and operated by John C. Stenger, and the other by John Volk. The Stenger distillery was located just east of town on the left side of the road on property which was owned by Eugene Feller. This property was the John C. Stenger property and his home is still there in a bad state of repair. (Figure 7 & 7A) Figure 7 is a picture of his house in 1875 and Figure 7A is a picture of the flour mill he operated.

Figure 7

ST. LEON GRIST & SAW MILLS, J.C.STENGER & A.BISCHOFF PROPS- RES. OF J.C.STENGER, ST LEON, DEARBORN CO. IND

Figure 7A

This property, I have been told, has since been purchased by personnel from St. Joseph's church for future use. When I returned to St. Leon in October, 2013 to get more information for this book, I was told that the building had been destroyed. At one time, along with the Joseph and Mary Bulach house, it was one of the finest in St. Leon.

The Volk distillery was located north of St. Leon toward Southgate on land owned by Albert Volk at the time of this writing. Its approximate location was 100 yards south of the Volk house. I visited him and interviewed him and he still had the stamps which were used on the whiskey barrels.

The winery was owned and operated by Joseph Stenger, who is the older brother of John C. Stenger. Dick Stenger, who is a descendant of Joseph, reported that his 96 year old cousin, Sister Evangelita of Notre Dame SND visited and recalled the workings of the winery. There was a huge trough in which the grapes were placed and a heavy log would be lowered to crush the grapes. The first press of juice always went to the church and the other presses were sold as wine to local citizens.

The location of the winery was east of St. Leon and on the left side of the road. It was the first piece of property east of St. Joseph's church. At the time of this writing that property was owned by Al Glaub. This property has since been purchased by St. Joseph's Church personnel. The next property south and on the left was the distillery owned by his brother John.

Of the three ice houses, one was owned by John Schuman and another by Joe Hoffman. John Schuman used the ice to cool beer sold in his tavern. It is believed that Joe Hoffman sold ice to other tavern owners. The third ice house was owned by a group of individuals. They were Bill Frey, John Andres, John Frey, August Frey, Joseph Schuman, and Joseph Kraus. They made ice for their own personal use. Joseph Kraus was my grandfather and he explained how they cut and stored the ice.

The site for their ice house was at the crossroads of Schuman and Kraus roads just east of East Central High School. I recall fishing in this shallow pond in the late 1940's. Because it was shallow it froze easily. This group of individuals would cut the ice and store it in sawdust to be used during the summer. They also let this ice be used at the annual church picnics at St. Joseph's church. I recall seeing them remove ice from the sawdust during the church picnic. I was probably 10 years old at that time.

That pond is no longer there as it was bulldozed and made level for the Hoosier Foreign Auto Service. This is an auto mechanic service run by Duane Bischoff. He is the son of Leroy Bischoff and brother of Danny Bischoff who runs the bike shop on US # 46 where Alig's service station used to be.

One of the two cider mills was owned and operated by Henry Wilhelm. It was located west of St. Leon and east of the house now owned by Bob and Rita Wilhelm Gesell. The other was owned by another Wilhelm, and it was located south of St. Leon on the same site as the present fire station. It was later owned by his son-in-law Oswald Lobenstein. In the late 40's this mill was very much in demand. The lines of wagons with apples and barrels for the cider were longer than a football field. After his death, his grandchildren Dennis and James Callahan operated it for a few years. It ceased operation in the 1950's. It was torn down when the fire station was built.

As a child I always went there for the first day of operation to get some apple juice. It did not become cider until it fermented. Normally the alcohol content of fermented cider was 3-5% depending on the sugar content of the apples. The first day for making cider was quite a community event. The wagons with their apples were lined up, and they would gather round and talk while they waited for their apples to get pressed. Oswald would grind them up and press them to squeeze out the juice. It was amazing to watch him. There would be hundreds of honey bees flying around to get honey off the juice and the apple pulp, but he never seemed to mind. The juice would go into a container or 50 gallon barrel. My father always took enough apples to get enough juice to fill a 50 gallon barrel.

It was normal for the farmers to bring their own barrels and some brought two 50 gallon barrels. If you went to the basement of a farm house, you would normally find 3-5 50 gallon barrels of cider, vinegar, and wine. Keep in mind that they had their own orchards and vineyards and could make their own alcoholic beverages. The barrels were bought from a local barrel maker and later from Seagram's distillery in Lawrenceburg, IN.

The barrels from Seagram's were used whiskey barrels that had a charred inside and residual whiskey. This added a little flavor to wine or cider. It also served somewhat as a preservative. Because cider had a very low alcohol percentage, some farmers made a drink called "applejack" which increased alcohol percentage considerably. It was done by adding raisins to the cider and refermenting it.

The two breweries were owned by a Bischoff and a person whom everyone knew as Old Leonard. Old Leonard's brewery was located about a half block south of town. Joe Schuman built a garage over this same location. The garage is still operational and is run by Joe's son Walter and some his children. It was reported by Joe that while digging for the foundation for the garage, they found the foundation of the old brewery.

The sorghum and molasses mill was located south of town and was owned and operated by John Merkl. The mill was later purchased by Henry Wedding and moved west of St. Leon near the crossroads of the American Legion.

The first flour mill was built around 1818 by the Lawrence family about three miles west of St. Leon on Tanner's Creek. [4] It was near the point where US #46 crosses the creek. The second flour mill was built in 1855 by Henry, Joseph, and John C. Stenger.[4] It was later owned by John C. Stenger and Alois Bischoff. This mill ceased operation in 1896. (Figure 7A) It was a huge structure with three dams for the three mill ponds. It was a block north of town on land later owned by Florian Weldishofer.

I used to hunt rabbits with my dad and brother Wes in this area, and I recall seeing the ruins of the old structure in the late 40's. The ruins of this building were torn down, but visual evidence of the mill ponds can still be seen. At the present time trees are growing on these dams and they are hard to define. The town trustees have purchased land for a park on or near this site.

It was hard to determine the exact number of sawmills because ownership changed quite often. For example, the sawmill located across the county line on US #1toward Southgate was owned by Earl Wilhelm at the time of this writing. It was bought from Pete Andres. Pete bought it from Al Knecht, who bought it from Adam Rippberger. When Al Knecht owned the mill it was located west of St. Leon on the hill adjoining the Jerry Bulach farm. John C. Stenger also built a sawmill in 1854, but the location of that mill is unknown.[2]

Jeremiah Watkins built the first saw mill in the St. Leon area in 1815. It was located along SR #1 about two and half miles south of town. This sawmill was later operated by Charlie Schaeffer. Another sawmill was built by John C. Stenger in 1954.[5] At the time of this writing, the sawmill built by Watkins was still operational in this location. The owner and operator was Raymond Alig. He was a huge man and very muscular. As a kid growing up I heard about feats of strength between him and William Schuman. One story was a bet about who could lift the front end of an International truck. According to what I was told, both were able to pick it off the ground.

There were three known brickyards in St. Leon, and it is thought there was a fourth. One brickyard was owned by Al Knecht, and he also operated a sawmill on the same site. It was about one block west of St. Leon. There was a house there for many years and in the 40's and 50's it was owned by John and Lena Weldishofer Bulach. John was the son of Joseph Bulach who built the grocery store and tavern in the center of town. They were also my grandparents. On my way home from school, I often stopped at their house for a cookie or snack. I recall seeing all the brick fragments in their barnyard as I crossed the field to my parent's house which was across the creek and on the next hill west.

Another brickyard was located east of St. Leon on the left side of the road. It was just west of the road going down to the conservation club. The third brickyard was north of town on the Robert Frey farm, later purchased by his son Edward. The fourth brickyard is thought to have been on the Jerry Bulach farm just west of St. Leon. That farm was owned by Michael Newman and they built a huge brick home on that property. I was told that the bricks were soft and did not hold up very well. Joseph and Mary Schuler Bulach bought the farm in 1870 and sold it to their son John and Lena Weldishofer Bulach. They sold it their son Clarence and Bertha Kraus Bulach. They sold it to their son Jerry, who is the current owner. That home was destroyed in the 1930's, and the current home on that location was built. (Figure 8)

Wagon shops and blacksmith shops were often synonymous. Ed Kraus had a wagon and blacksmith shop in Schaffenburg near the site where Joe Alig had a service station west of town on US #46. This blacksmith shop was moved by Billy Wuestefeld. I talked to him in 1967 and he showed it to me. As of this writing in 2013, I have no idea what became of it. Another wagon maker in the 1850's was Louis Moster. He also made and had on hand all kinds of coffins.[2] Joseph Schuman purchased a blacksmith shop in the 1890's. It is quite likely that it was the same shop owned by Louis Moster.[5]

Figure 8

Figure 9

One of Moster's competitors during this period was John C. Stenger. He started a blacksmith shop in 1848. It is believed that this shop was later owned by Henry Doerflein. His shop was located on land owned by Julian Ober and across the road from the St. Joseph's elementary school. In addition to blacksmithing, he also made and repaired machinery.[2] This building is still there (Figure 9). I visited Julian who is 88 years old, and he told me that it has been remodeled. He also told me that the building next to that one was used to make coffins.

John Hilbert was another wagon maker and his shop was located about a half block west of town on the left side of the road on land that was owned by Irwin Hilbert in 1967. That is the present site of the US # 1 bypass. John made and repaired all kinds of wagons. He sold the shop to the Stumpf brothers who converted it into a dance hall. According to stories only a few dances were held there.

The cigar manufacturers of St. Leon were Herman Wesseler and the Telcher families. The extent of their business is unknown. However, it has been said that the cigars they made were the forerunners of cigar called "San Felice." Their shop was located west of St. Leon near the first crossroad and north toward the farm once owned by Walter Wuestefeld.

The dentist of St. Leon was the blacksmith Henry Doerflein. I was told that Henry and his trusty pliers pulled many a tooth for residents who had nowhere else to go when a tooth needed pulling. Getting a tooth pulled in those days was quite different from today. There was no waiting room, no novocaine, and no needles. There was just a strong pair of arms and hands. One swift yank and it was over. I can only imagine a person's emotional state and how that must have felt.

Dick Stenger[1] interviewed his 95 year old cousin Sister Evangelita (Sisters of Notre Dame) and she recalled that her grandfather John H. Stenger also pulled teeth. He has made a DVD of that interview and copies of that can be purchased from him. I have watched that DVD and there is a lot of interesting footage of early St. Leon including a picture of the original parsonage with the graveyard in front. The only grave marker still there is the one of Valentine Lawrence.

The horticulturist of the St. Leon area was John Frey. He produced and marketed all kinds of domestic fruits, and his specialty was peaches. His business was a profitable one in the 1870's and 80's.[2]

During the wheat harvest season, threshing machine owners were very busy. There were three or four threshing machines that were used to separate the straw from the wheat. The cost of buying a threshing machine was usually more than one person could afford. Citizens who had part ownership in threshing machines were the following: Al Geis, Al Knecht, Joe Schuler, Joe Zimmer, John Frey, Frank Frey, Louis Kuebel, John Andres, Philip Alig, George Werner, Albert Bishop and John Wilhelm.

With the advent of combines, threshing machines became obsolete. A person who was somewhat of a collector of obsolete equipment was Everet Hoover. He owned the old airport hangar on US # 46 next to the Schuman farm and Joe Alig's service station. In the 1960's and 70's he restored old steam engines, tractors, threshing machines, etc. I recall as a youngster in the early 50's taking a ride in small airplane when the hanger opened. The airstrip ran north from US # 46 to the road west of the crossroads in St. Leon. It was a dirt airstrip. The airstrip and hanger saw little activity and when it closed, it was purchased by Mr. Hoover. This hanger has since been remodeled. (Figure 10)

Figure 10

Mention was made earlier about the illegal business of moonshining. St. Leon area was noted for good moonshine. It was a very profitable business and that is the reason why so many citizens became moonshiners. In the early 20's, a gallon of good moonshine would sell for as much as $22.00/gallon. During the 1930's, because the supply of moonshine had increased, as more and more citizens produced it, the price had dropped to $4.00/gallon. I was told that moonshine from St. Leon had a wide market. People from all parts of Indiana and Ohio came to St. Leon to buy moonshine. It seems that the Germans of St. Leon were very good at making good moonshine.

The early producers of moonshine made their product in the open. No one tried to hide that they were making it. That all changed in the 30's when revenuers cracked down on moonshining. Many gave up the practice, but a few continued the practice and had to be very careful not to get caught. As mentioned earlier, one moonshiner hid his still in a sinkhole and covered it with brush. Others used straw stacks, hay maws, and wood piles.

Straw stacks were a fixture on every farm prior to the invention of balers. They were huge mounds of straw 20-30 feet high and 30-40 feet in diameter. Straw stacks had many uses. Birds would make holes in them and build their nests there. I remember shooting 30-40 in one night with my BB gun for the pest contest put on by the Future Farmers of America at Sunman High School. The straw was used for bedding in the barns.

There was a special tool with a hook that was used to pull straw out of the stack. I also used to just sit down and lie against the stack and let the sun warm me and just do nothing but relax. I wonder how many other farm kids did the same thing. Moonshiners found that it was easy to create a cave in a straw stack to hide their still. I don't think many moonshiners used a straw stack to hide their still. The danger of fire in a straw stack had to be very real.

In reflection, it is hard to believe that all of these businesses existed in a town as small as St. Leon. Keep in mind that citizens had to produce everything locally because trips to larger cities would take a day or longer. So all of these businesses were created and were successful in supplying their needs. The citizens of St. Leon were those who operated these businesses and the farmers who supported the businesses.

Figure 10A shows a layout of St. Leon as it existed in 1875. You can see Joe Bulach's store and post office and the location of many of the other businesses. It is interesting to note all the businesses on the right side of US # 1. When I was growing up, the only one left was the Oswald Lobenstein cider mill and the Basil Bruder Cooperage. The Bruder building and house still exist and is currently owned by Jerry and Arlene Bulach Wilgenbush. (Figure 10B & 10C)

When the industrial revolution reached the Midwest in the late 1800's and the cost of living rose, many citizens couldn't make a living on their small farms. Many of the factories were too far away for them to commute to work so they moved to cities to be closer to work. The lack of railroad access for St. Leon discouraged the expansion of local businesses. A trend toward bigness was also growing and small businesses such as cigar makers, wagon makers, distillers, etc. were driven out of business. The result was that after 1885, no new businesses were formed, and those that were already established began a slow decline. The outflow of citizens to the factories, and the inflow of cheaper products and manufactured goods caused population to decline and businesses to deteriorate.

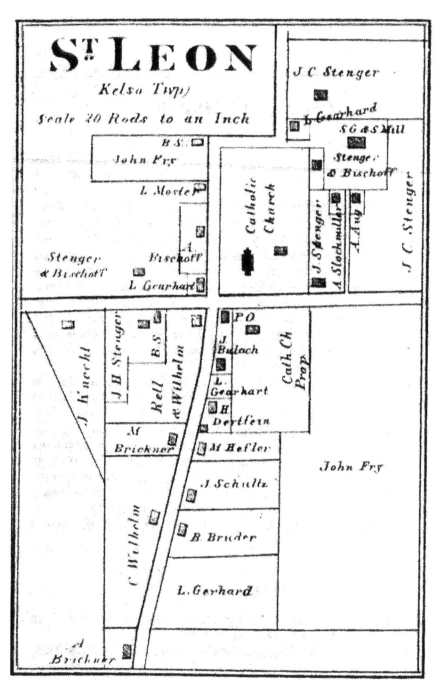

Figure 10A

Figure 10B

Figure 10C

Businesses in 1967

Since the original writing of this history in 1967 much has happened in the St. Leon area. At that time (1967) there were a few businesses in the area and a brief description of them is the following:

Schuman's General Store and Tavern carried a complete line of International Harvester equipment, groceries, work clothes, shoes, hardware, grains, and feeds of all kinds. This store is now a tavern that serves food and spirits and was described earlier.

Walter Schuman's Garage specialized in the repair of International Harvester equipment. He also is an excellent mechanic and can basically repair anything mechanical. This garage is still operational and is run Walter and Mary's boys Don, Ron, and Mike. His son Ron also has a wrecker service at this location.

Jake Stenger's Garage repairs all kinds of machinery, automobiles, trucks, and any other mechanical piece of equipment. Most of the repairs are made by Joseph Andres. He is an excellent mechanic and has been practicing his trade since his return from military service in the Korean conflict. Jake Stenger is the owner and operator of the garage and he assists with some mechanical work. In addition to repairs he also sold gasoline at this location. That garage is no longer operational and the building is owned by Eric Stenger. (Figure 5A)

Joe Alig's Service Station was on US # 46 just west of St. Leon. Joe Alig's station also sold tires, had a pin ball machine on which the locals spent a lot of time on. He also sold hamburgers which many of us kids at the time thought were wonderful. He had one of the first refrigerators and fresh ground beef was something many of us kids did not get at home. He also had a back room where we could go and play cards. There was no TV back then and going to Joe's to play cards, play the pin ball machine, and have a hamburger was something we really enjoyed. Joe was a great person and he tolerated our shenanigans.

Figure 11

He closed that station and built the Shell station on US #1 and I 74. The current building on US #46 (Figure 11) is now a bike shop owned and operated by Daniel

Bischoff. Daniel is the son of Leroy Bischoff. Leroy married Francis Beneker who was the daughter of Amos Beneker. Amos and my father were great friends in their early years. My dad often talked about the year in the early 1900's when they drove their Model T Ford to Iowa and got jobs as hired hands to shuck corn and other farm labor jobs.

Irvin Fuernstein's Service Station. Irvin was the owner and operator of the third service station. He was a bachelor and he also catered to us juveniles. One never knew what he was going to do next at his station. At one time or another he had a restaurant, sold smokes, fixed radios, TV's etc. (See earlier picture of this station) This station is currently being run by Ken and Faye Fuernstein French.

Werner's General Store. Virgil Werner had a small general store on his farm just west of the American Legion. He would go to Cincinnati and buy produce and products for sale at reduced prices. You might say he was the original Big Lots.

Earl Wilhelm Saw Mill. It was located just across the county line toward Southgate. When this was operated by John Wilhelm, it was one of the largest in the area. This mill was bulldozed when the new US # 1 was built. Prior to the new highway, there was a sharp turn separating the county lines. The saw mill was on the left as you crossed the county line.

Leo Wilhelm Saw Mill. This is located just west of Southgate and is still operational. Leo's sons and descendants have expanded this mill a great deal. This saw mill was the most productive of the four sawmills in the St. Leon area. With the help of his sons he produced and sold a lot of lumber.

I recall visiting that mill one day to find a good piece of white oak. I was an assistant principal at a school in Cincinnati, and I needed a piece of white oak to make a paddle. Back in those days, paddling students who needed discipline was allowed. I had broken many paddles and was told that white oak paddles would not split. I still have that paddle.

Carl Hoog Saw Mill. This mill was the last to be built, but with the help of his sons he seems to be doing well.

Raymond Alig Saw Mill. He operates the one his father Phillip owned. He has a large operation and employs a few locals to assist his operation. At one time, my brother Jerry worked for him. That mill is no longer operational. This concludes writing about the businesses that existed in the 1960's. Another important part of the History of St. Leon is the post office.

The Post Office and Naming the Town

This town was named St. Joe's until sometime in the 1850's, according to Father Ebnet's unfinished history. He had found an 1853 baptismal record signed by Father Moschal that included the words St. Leon. We also know that John C. Stenger was St. Leon's first postmaster and he was appointed to that position on October 2nd, 1852. In order for the federal government to create a post office for a town, it had to have a name. According to Ebnet's history, a parishioner by the name of Nicholas Ratz related what his father Mathew had told him about how St. Leon got its name.

When they first applied for a name, St. Joseph was the one that used on the application. It was rejected because there was already a St. Joseph in existence in Indiana. The men met in Joseph Stenger's store east of the church and rectory to discuss another name. Several names suggested were "Wilhelm's Corner" and "Aschaffenburg." This was the name of a southern city in Bavaria, Germany. If you recall, I mentioned a settlement about a mile away called Schaffenburg. So that might have been a good choice, but most citizens thought it was too long for the name of the town.

The name St. Leo was suggested because he was a pope who had visited Germany and they felt good about that name. That was the name sent in to name the town for the new post office. The person who sent in the application had embellished the "O" with an extra curve on the end. The person receiving the application read it to mean "Leon." So the town getting the new post office was St. Leon, and the citizens decided to accept it.

At that time there was no rural route mail service. Mail was brought from the New Trenton Post Office by horseback to St. Leon. According to a conversation with Wilfred Bischoff, his grandfather rode his horse to get the mail. The road to Trenton is the same road alongside their house and the one that goes to the Conservation

Club. He would get the mail and take it to the post office. Anyone wanting their mail had to come to the post office to get it. Each postmaster had the post office in their home or place of business. John C. Stenger in 1852 became the first postmaster, and Joseph Bulach in 1860 became the 2nd postmaster.

He served until June 23, 1876. He had become very ill with tuberculosis and died on May 3rd of that year. His untimely death at the age of 43 was a severe loss for the leadership of the town. He and his wife Mary were very involved in the community with the church and the store. They also helped farmers sell their produce with their huckster route. I was told they had many parties at the ballroom of their big brick house just west of town.

The following are the postmasters who served after him:

- Patrick Diver 1876 to 1881
- Christopher Meder 1881 to 1888
- Andrew Aug 1888 and succeed by his widow to 1901
- Alois Knecht 1901 to 1908
- George Doerflein 1908 to 1909.
- Caroline Lobenstein 1909 to 1934
- Rose Schuman 1934 to 1955

The post office for Caroline Lobenstein was a small room on the right side of the house about one block south of town at the residence of Anna Mae Dierckman Callahan (Figure 12) .The post office for Rose Schuman is across the road and due west of the church (See Figure 2). As a child I went there often because she also sold ice cream and penny candy. She was a very nice lady and everyone just loved going into that post office. With the closing of that post office, the St. Leon community was served by rural routes.

Figure 12

The above description of businesses and the post office was written in 1967. I also wrote at that time that water and sewer were being talked about. That has already happened. The US #1 bypass has also taken place. Next on the horizon will be what happens to St. Joseph's Parish. There is talk about creating a mega church and merging four parishes. There would then be only one church for the parishioners of all four parishes. St. Joseph's Church would no longer be used. What a tragedy that would be? This church has been the focus for St. Leon since it was built in 1861. Much has changed in St. Leon and the changes will keep coming? I predict there will be a shopping mall somewhere near the US #1 and I-74 exit in the not too distant future?

References

1. Dick Stenger, 477 Riddle Road, Mount Healthy, Ohio 45231 dickstenger@netzero.com.
2. History of Dearborn County, 1915.
3. Fette, A. (1951). History of New Alsace.
4. History of Dearborn and Ohio Counties, 1885.
5. Atlas of Indiana, 1875.

Chapter VI

Education in St. Leon

Prior to 1850, schools in Indiana communities were established in this manner. A trustee would call a meeting for the purpose of building a school house. Some communities levied a fine of 37 cents a day for those not wishing to help build the school house. The building, nevertheless, had to fulfill certain state requirements. It could be built out stone, hewn timber, frame, or brick. There had to be eight feet between the floors and the first floor had to be one foot above the ground. It had to be furnished in a manner calculated to make the students and teacher comfortable.[1] If you will note that the word "teacher" is singular, you will also realize that these early schools were one room school houses.

After the school house was built, another meeting of the trustees was called, and they had to decide how many months the school would operate. How to support the school and the teacher also had to be decided? They had to levy a tax, charge tuition, or find some other means. They then had to decide to interview and hire a teacher. If they found him/her to be qualified in the 3rs they issued a certificate that said this person was a qualified teacher.[1]

Those citizens who sent their kids to this school had to pay the teacher. The early teachers saw little money and payment was usually in the form of commodities needed by the teacher and his/her family. Teachers were often underpaid and there were competent teachers, incompetent ones, and so I have been told, some were downright mean.[2] In those days, if you could read, write, and do arithmetic; you were qualified to be a teacher. All you had to do was find someone to hire you.

The Early Schools

After 1850, the State of Indiana had some funds available for education. With this extra source of income, more schools were built, and by 1876 there were five schools serving students in the St. Leon community. They were located in the center of Section 15, the S.W. corner of Section 3, the N.W. corner of Section 12, the S.W. corner of Section 13 and the church school within city limits. The school in Section 15 was the first school built. That occurred in 1832 and it was located about a quarter mile south of the dogleg on Dogridge Road near the Ellen Bulach residence. At one time as many as 70 students attended school there. For those who are not familiar with the area, this is about a half mile south of East Dearborn High School. Dogridge Road was renamed Trojan Road from US 46 to East Central then it becomes Dogridge Road again.

Three schools were built in this area. It was one of the more populated areas in the St. Leon area and was probably served by the Schaffenburg community about a mile from the St. Leon city limits. Settlement in this area occurred because of its proximity to Tanner's Creek. This road at one time went all the way to New Alsace and crossed Tanners Creek at the end of Dogridge Road. The second school was built around 1850 and the third school was built across Dogridge Road where it makes the first dogleg. This school was called the Wintzinger School and later the Hyland School after the names of the teachers.

The third school was built in 1865, and it also was known as the Hyland School. This school was closed sometime in the late 1930's. It was named after Bill Hyland, who was the son of the earlier John Hyland. John taught in the second school for eight years, and Bill taught for 20 consecutive years in the third brick one room school house. When I wrote this history in 1967, that structure was still standing. Joe Herzog had it torn down to make room for his subdivision sometime in the 70's. It stood on the right side of Leona Drive and the left side of Dogridge Road.

This school closed because of improved roads and the popularity of the Catholic Church school in St. Leon. Since most citizens were Catholic, they preferred sending them to this school where students went to church each morning as part of their school experience. When attendance at the Hyland School declined to a few students those doors were closed.

I visited Bill Hyland on his farm to talk him about that. He told me that he loved that school and hated closing it. His farm is still owned by three Hylands, who are sons of Victor Hyland who is a descendant of Bill Hyland. The original house still stands although it has been remodeled several times. It is located on the left side of Hyland Road about a half mile west of US #1.

Figure 1

I had no information on the location of the fifth school. It is possible that it was the one room school house in Southgate. That school still exists (Figure 1) and is owned and has been preserved by Max and Patty McLeary. In the late 1800's and early 1900's, Southgate like St. Leon, was a very active community. There were stores and mills, and a weigh station for weighing cattle. As a kid we went to the mill to have feed ground for the animals. The Schucks owned the general store and mill and lived in a grand brick home right on the crossroads at US #1. That house is now in ruins.

There was also a baseball field. It was the only baseball field in the area and, according to Max McLeary, a Cincinnati Reds farm team once played there. I recall as a boy watching my dad pitch on that ball field. That ball field was located east of town and right behind the weigh station. The weigh station was used by local farmers to weigh their cattle when they were sold to buyers. These buyers would come around and buy cattle from local farmers. I recall my dad making a bet with the buyer on the weight of the cow being bought. Then it would be off to Southgate to see who won the bet.

The First Catholic School

The first Catholic school in St. Leon was built in 1856. It was built during Father Koering's pastorate and some teachers were nuns from the Sisters of St. Francis.[3] Usually, a man taught in conjunction with the nuns. Two of the men teachers at this school were Holloman and Schiffer.

The boys and girls were separated and the nuns taught the girls and the men taught the boys. Whether this was done to keep the sexes separated or for religious reasons is unknown. It could have been done because the boys were too difficult to handle. Somehow I doubt that because I was taught by nuns and they could terrify you just by looking at you. This practice of teaching boys and girls separately was discontinued in 1885. After this date, men ceased to teach in St. Joseph's School, and boys and girls were taught in the same classroom.[3]

The second Catholic School was built in 1865, and at the time of this writing in 1967, that structure still existed. (Figure 2) At one time it was a residence for Louise and Lawrence Schuman who operated the tavern and grocery store next door. It was a solid stone two story structure. The second floor was the school and the first floor was the living quarters for the nuns. In 1885 when St. Leon's population was at its peak, there were 120 students attending this two story school. It became so crowded that some students were taught on the first floor. The overflow of students was taught in the Old Leonard House where Jake's Garage now stands. That garage is no longer operational and the building is owned by Eric Stenger. (Figure 3)

Figure 2

Figure 3

82

The Current Two Room School and Expansion

The third and present school was built in 1928. It was a two room structure with a stairwell in the middle and full basement underneath. One side was for grades 1-4 and the other for grades 5-8. Adjacent to this school was the living quarters for the St. Francis nuns. It was built the same year by Oscar Stenger at a cost of $19,823.29. Both structures still exist although the school has been expanded and has a large kitchen and dining facility that can be rented by citizens for reunions, and other gatherings. (Figure 4)

Figure 4

I spent all 8 years of my elementary school education at this school, and it prepared me well for life.

Aside from the education we received from the nuns there were other interesting things that happened. One was recess where students could go outside and compete against each other. A favorite activity was red rover, red rover come over, where students would charge a line of students to see if they could break through. Wrestling was another favorite where students would wrestle each other to see who could make the other say "I give." Both of these activities would be forbidden in schools today, but in the 1950's it was very acceptable.

Another interesting thing about this school was the latrine/toilet facilities. This was a wooden structure adjacent to the school. One side was for the girls and the other for the boys. As I recall, there were 4-6 places or holes where you could go to the bathroom. When I graduated from the grade 1-4 side of the school to the grade 5-8, I was told by an 8th grade student that if I stuck my head down one of the holes I would be able to see the girl's side of the latrine. Many a student, stuck their head down a hole hoping to see something on the other side. Unfortunately, there was a wooden barrier that extended down to prevent anyone seeing what was happening on the other side. This was a standard prank that was played on all entering 5th grade students.

The attendance at St. Joseph's school has varied a great deal over the years from a high of 120 in 1885[4] to a low of 47s in 1950. Attendance by date and year are the following:[5]

1910, 100 students
1926, 64 students
1935, 88 students (50 boys and 38 girls)
1940, 71 students (33 boys and 38 girls)

1950, 47 students (33 boys and 14 girls)
1962, 95 students (46 boys and 55 girls)

The last year of operation for this school was 1972. After that year all students attended public schools in Dearborn County.

It is surprising to note that the St. Joseph's School was a public school operated by the Catholic Church and taught by nuns of the St. Francis Order. Catholics and Protestants alike attended school here. Some Protestants, however, did not attend school until catechism and church attendance were over. St. Joseph's School was an excellent example of the harmony that can exist between people of different faiths.

The school was supported by State of Indiana funds even though students were given religious instructions. I recall one day when the superintendent of schools for Dearborn County visited our school to inspect. The nuns were careful to hide all the catechism books during the visit. With today's legal systems and the overabundance of lawyers, that could not happen. It is unknown when this practice started, but it is thought to have been between 1861 and 1874. It was during these dates that the St. Leon Corporation was formed. The pastor during these dates was Father Scheidler. He was the one responsible for forming the corporation so he could get State funds for the school. State support for St. Joseph's School began with the forming of the corporation. I have no record of when State support was stopped.

References

1. Dunn, Jacob. 1919. *Indiana and Indianans,* American Historical Society. V II, p. 869.
2. *History of Dearborn County,* 1915, p. 455.
3. *The Indiana Catholic Record.* P.110.
4. *History of Dearborn and Ohio Counties,* 1885, p. 581.
5. Church records kept in the rectory.

Chapter VII

St. Joseph's Church History

The church history of St. Leon began in the 1840's. During these years, a Catholic church and a Lutheran Church were established. In 1841, Rev. Joseph Ferneding established St. Joseph's Catholic Church. Prior to this date, citizens attended church at St. John's Church at Dover. If a priest visited St. Leon, mass was held in the school house east of town.[1]

In 1843, the German Evangelical Lutheran Church was established just west of Schaffenburg on US # 46. That structure still exists although services are seldom held there. It is a limestone structure built out of stone from a quarry on Tanners Creek. (Figure 1) I visited the cemetery in 1967 and found a tombstone for a civil war veteran, but no longer remember his name.

Figure 1

The Log Chapel

The Catholic Church in St. Leon was built of logs and it was a chapel. Prior to 1841, the Catholics of St. Leon attended services in Dover. Sometimes a priest was in the area and services were held in the school house. In 1841, as a result of the influence and encouragement of Rev. Joseph Ferneding , the citizens of St. Leon bought one and one quarter acres of land and erected the log chapel structure.[2] The location of that chapel is in the northwest corner of the existing cemetery. There is a cross marker where it stood. (Figure 2) The trustees who purchased that land were Henry Knote, Peter Renner, Henry Stenger, Peter Wilhelm, and Jacob Wilhelm. According to records in the recorder's office of the Dearborn County Courthouse, this land was bought from Nathaniel Towsley, and the deed was made out to these five trustees.

Figure 2

88

This was an error on the part of the trustees. The deed should have been made out to Bishop Hailandiere. It is the custom for all church land to be owned by the clergyman in charge of the diocese, and at that time the bishop was in charge. When he learned that the deed to the newly established parish was not in his name, he became very angry. Another factor that contributed to his anger was that he had not been consulted about forming the new parish. There were already three Catholic parishes within a few miles of each other: Dover was 2-3 miles, New Alsace was 5-6 miles, and Cedar Grove was 4-5 miles. He did not see a need for a new parish in the middle of existing parishes.

When Father Ferneding told the bishop that he had formed a new parish, at what was then called St. Joe, the bishop would not give his approval. He was visiting the parish at New Alsace at that time, and prior to his departure he did give his approval to build a chapel there. His approval contained a stipulation that the deed be put in his name and that the Catholics of St. Joe consider the Cross-Roads Church at Dover as their parish church (Stenger, 1991).

According to land records at the courthouse in Lawrenceburg, IN, Henry Stenger, Peter Wilhelm, and Peter Renner transferred one and nineteen hundreds of an acre of land to the bishop. The deed was put in Bishop Hailandiere's name on October 7th, 1846.

Father Ferneding was quite upset over the way the bishop had handled the creation of the parish at St. Joe's. He had organized and established many parishes in the area including New Alsace, Yorkville, St. Peter's, Lawrenceburg, Dover, Oldenburg, St. Nicholas, and

Milhousen. (Fette (1951) All of these parishes owe their beginnings to Father Ferneding. The disapproval of his actions in forming the new parish at St. Joe's caused him to resign his position and request to be transferred to the Cincinnati Diocese.

He spent his remaining years in the Cincinnati Diocese and is buried in the cemetery in St. Bernard, OH. According to the Stenger account of St. Joseph's Parish, he was born Oldenburg, Germany in 1802 and arrived in Cincinnati in 1832. He was ordained in 1833 and began his work establishing parishes in southeastern Indiana. In 1837 at St. Joe's, he baptized Peter Schmitt, Florian Frey, Jacob Wilhelm, Joseph Hahn, Henry Roell, Peter Renner, Peter Wilhelm, and Frank Knecht. His departure from the Vincennes Diocese was a great loss.

Father Ferneding was a positive influence on the growth of St. Joe's (St. Leon) while Bishop Hailandiere was a negative influence. Because of Father Ferneding, St. Leon is a Catholic community. Less than a mile away and near Schaffenburg, there was a Lutheran church, which could have attracted many Lutheran Germans from northern Germany. Instead St. Leon became a Catholic community that attracted immigrants from the Catholic part of southern Germany. There was a great influx of Catholics and in the 1940's and 1950's, there was only one family that was not Catholic. That family was the Oehlman family who lived on a turkey farm south of St. Leon. Without the establishment of the church in St. Leon, it may have ceased to exist like South Gate, Hubbels Corner, and Highland Center. These locations are still there, but they are no longer thriving communities.

Bishop Hailandiere and his actions were very detrimental to the growth of St. Leon.* According to Fette (1951), "The early growth and national expansion of St. Leon was considerably impeded and slowed in its infancy by Bishop Hailandiere's insistence on rigid discipline." (p.142) He was opposed to a parish consisting of one ethnic group, such as the Germans or Irish. He felt that a parish of one ethnic group would mean the needless multiplication of priests and buildings. That would result in a loss of revenue for parishes that had already been established.

* At this time St. Leon was still called St. Joe's. I will explain how it got the name St. Leon in a later chapter.

These were his intentions when he decreed that St. Leon should have a chapel and not a church. Without a church, the citizens of St. Leon would not have a pastor. They would have to go to church in nearby Dover, thereby increasing their revenues and congregation. Needless to say, he was not successful in his efforts because St. Leon became a German parish and Dover became an Irish parish. The bishop's reasoning seemed logical, but according to Blanchard (1898), the good bishop was lacking in executive abilities, and he resigned in 1887.

A side note about the Dover parish. According to stories I heard as kid, this town was settled by the workers who constructed the Whitewater Canal. The Whitewater Canal, which was built between 1836 and 1847, spanned a distance of seventy-six miles and stretched from Lawrenceburg, Indiana on the Ohio River through Brookville to Hagerstown, Indiana. The workers were Irish immigrants and they were great workers who were willing to do a back breaking job. Parts of the Whitewater Canal can still be seen near Brookville, IN. It is also interesting to note that relationships between the Irish in Dover and Germans in St. Leon could have been better, so I was told. The Germans in St. Leon sort of thought they were better than the Irish in Dover.

Land Purchases for the Church

The land for St. Joseph's Parish was acquired gradually and from different owners. Land purchases were made from 1841 to 1941. In 1841, the five trustees mentioned earlier, bought one and one fourth acres from Nathaniel Towsley for $23.00. This land includes much of the present cemetery. On May 22, 1842, John Folk sold four acres for $80.00. This is the land where the present church, school, and playground were built. John Stenger sold one and two thirds acre in 1844 and another acre was purchased from a St. Joseph's trust fund in 1846.[3] In 1931, according to Father Ebnet, Catherine Stenger sold a fifth of an acre for five dollars.

Since the establishment of the log chapel in 1841, St. Joseph's church has had many pastors. As mentioned earlier, the first was Father Ferneding, to whom the citizens of St. Leon will forever remain indebted. Because of Bishop Hailandiere's decree, St. Joseph's Parish did not have a resident pastor. The congregation was served by neighboring pastors. There was Father O'Rourke and Father Bennett from Dover, Father Engeln from St. Peter's, and Father Stahl from New Alsace.[2]

The Construction of St. Joseph's Church

The corner stone was laid in 1859 under the leadership of Father Koering. The old log chapel was too small for the growing congregation. The limestone foundation for the 56 by120 foot church came from local quarries. One such quarry was on the Mason farm near Tanner's Creek off of Dogridge Road. The bricks came from local brickyards (described earlier) with most of them coming from the Frey brickyard, just north of town. The construction workers were housed and fed by Joe and Mary Bulach who owned the tavern and grocery store across the road.

The architecture of the church is predominantly Gothic. This is the church architecture that is typical of southern Germany. A German historian wrote the following about German Gothic architecture: "The Gothic master builder used pointed arches instead of the semicircular ones . . . increasingly large stained glass windows... the façade became the dominating part of the building...the interior...has a huge hall and side aisles." (Reinhardt, 1978 p.150.) Typical of Gothic church architecture was a tall steeple. More information about the stained glass windows, altars, and other church adornments can be found in the Stenger history of the church.

This description of Gothic Church architecture is typical for what you find when you look at St. Joseph's Church. All of the arches are pointed and the slanting roof enhances the effect. There are many stained glass windows and the interior of the church is like a huge hall and has a side aisle on each side. Of course the 120 foot church steeple is gone and the exterior appearance of the church no longer resembles Gothic architecture. Compare the appearance of the church in 1885 on the back cover with the appearance of the church in 1865 (Figure 1A) and the present church on the front cover.

St. Joseph's Church.
Dearborn ... Ind.

Figure 1A

The Pastors of St. Joseph's Church

In 1853, Bishop St. Palais lifted Bishop Hailandiere's decree that the parishioners of St. Joseph's church attend the church at Dover. In that year St. Joseph's Church got their first resident pastor. His name was Father Moschall and he was born in the Alsace-Lorraine region of Germany in 1819 (Stenger, 1991). He was followed by Father Arnold Pinkers in 1854 and Father Henry Koering in 1855.

Father Koering remained as the pastor for five years until 1860. During his pastorate a number of major changes occurred. In 1856, he erected a school, and in 1859, he laid the cornerstone for the present church. According to Fette (1951), he was very disheartened by the slow progress being made in building the church. He left and went to the Cincinnati Diocese. He also requested nuns from the Sisters of St. Francis at Oldenburg to teach the 50+ students at the new school. This began the teaching of students by nuns from the Oldenburg order which continued for many more years.

He was followed by Father Anthony Scheidler who took charge in November of 1860. He was born in Westphalia, Germany and St. Joseph's Church was his first pastorate (Blanchard, 1898). On his arrival, the parish was divided and in a state of disarray. Progress on the church was at a standstill. He succeeded in restoring order and finished building the church in 1861. (See Figure 1A) This is a drawing of the church, rectory, and surroundings in 1865. The two story Catholic School and Joseph and Mary Bulach's tavern and grocery story are on the left side of the road. The church and rectory are on the right side.

The church had a 120 foot church steeple that gave it a very graceful appearance. From the top of the spire/steeple one could see all the way to Harrison, OH. I know that to be a fact, because I went all the way to the top one morning when I was about 10 years old to see for myself. Other additions to the church were three bells for the steeple, the existing three altars, and a rectory.

He was a very organized and busy person. He also built a new school in 1865[4] and attended to the parishioners at St. John's in Dover from 1860-1870. At the Dover church he erected the stations, built the sanctuary, installed the organ, and in 1865, built a new brick two story schoolhouse.[4] He was also responsible for the sale of the old log church, the log schoolhouse, and the old rectory.

The old log church was sold at public auction on 9/4/1862. In Father Ebnet's History he wrote this about the sale: "This humble building that had witnessed times of joy and sorrow, where people knelt, prayed and drew spiritual comfort from the Source and Fountain of all Grace, was now dismantled and parts of it went in various directions to serve a new purpose in a new place." The logs, windows, and some boards were sold to Henry Roell.[1] According to hearsay, some of these logs were used to construct a general store owned by Ralph Schuck at South Gate.

He accomplished a great deal in a very short period of time. Perhaps he was too ambitious and too much of a change agent. I say this because the parishioners of St. Joseph's Church petitioned to have him relieved of his duties as pastor. Perhaps his accomplishments were too much of a drain on the resources of the parish.

The old log school house was sold and relocated about one mile east of St. Leon on the right side of the road. It was on the old Fischer place and was sometimes used for parties. The building was sometimes referred to as Beverly Hills. That building no longer exists.

The old rectory was a one and one half story frame structure. It was located on the same site as the present rectory. Because of its poor condition, the parishioners decided to sell it rather than have it repaired. The new rectory was built on the same location. The old rectory was bought by Henry Doerflein and moved to a block south of town in a space now occupied by the fire station.[1] The location of that building can be seen in Figure 10A in Chapter 5.

Father Scheidler's successor was Father John Gabriel who was born in Eunetbergen, Switzerland. His tenure was from 7/28/1874 till 9/16/1896. His tenure was very successful and included covering all necessary expenses, repairs, and improvements. He paid off the church debt and left behind a sum of $1600.00 to cover future expenses (Blanchard, 1898).

The next pastor of St. Joseph's Church was Father Feigen who was born in Baden, Germany in 1854. His tenure was from 1896 till 1902. During this time he had the church consecrated by Bishop Chatard on 9/8/1897, installed a new furnace in the church, added a new vestry, improved the main altar, and paid $1000.00 to have the church interior frescoed. (Figure 2A) It was a beautiful fresco, and I often marveled at it as child. The fresco was not restored and has since been painted over. He also built the present rectory at a cost of $4000.00. He died on 4/28/1902 and is buried in the church cemetery.

Figure 2A

The next pastor was Father Martin Andres who was born on 1/28/1855 in New Orleans, LA. His tenure was from 1902 till 1925. His reputation for the spiritual and material welfare of the parish was excellent. One of the writers of the 1915 Dearborn County History had this to say about Father Andres: "Great hearts there are also among men; they carry the volume of manhood; their presence is sunshine; their coming changes our climate; they oil the bearings of life; their shadow always behind them; and they make right living easy. Blessed are the happiness-makers. They represent the best forces in civilization. They are to the heart and home what the honeysuckle is to the door over which it clings."[5] Judging from this tribute and the comments of some of the older citizens in St. Leon during the 1960's when this was written, he was probably one of our best pastors. Of course when I was growing up, we had Father Ebnet, and he was also one of our best.

A number of pastors followed Father Andres and there is no record of what happened during their tenure. In order of succession these pastors were the following:[1]

- Father Gerhardstein 9/1925 till 6/1927.
- Father Loibl 7/1927 till 12/1929.
- Father Schenk 12/1929 till 12/1934.
- Father Mellen 1/1934 till 6/1935.
- Father Beacher 6/1935 till 2/1936.
- Father Wagner 3/1936 till 4/1936.
- Father Kabey 4/1936 till 7/1937.
- Father A. J. Ebnet 7/1937 till 1961.

Father Adam Joseph Ebnet was born at Delaware, IN on 12/24/1896. He was named after Father Adam Feigen who was the pastor of his parents' church in nearby Napoleon, IN. By coincidence Father Feigen was the pastor of St. Joseph's from 1896 till 1902. On Father Ebnet's arrival, he found the parish in a very run down condition, and there was no one on hand to greet him when he arrived.

He grew up in a German family that was used to taking care of things and he used these talents, acquired while growing up, to make many of the repairs needed in the parish. He was very frugal, thrifty, and industrious and during his pastorate, he managed to pay off the church debt. He also repaired all the buildings, replaced the church steeple, redecorated the church interior, and left a balance of $15,000.00.

He was very stern and businesslike and not loved by all, but he was nevertheless respected for his many good qualities. I was one of his servers for many years and he always treated us with a great deal of respect. He was easy to talk to if you had a problem. He was kind, sympathetic, an excellent manager, and best of all he loved his parish and parishioners. He was very interested in the parishes' past as well its present and future. His interest in the present is verified by the excellent condition in which he left it.

His interest in the past can be seen by his efforts to write the history of the parish. I spent many hours in the rectory going over his notes and records. He began his writings in the 1940's and hoped to present his history in 1961, which was the 100 year anniversary of the dedication of the church. Unfortunately, his weakened condition and subsequent death prevented him from accomplishing this goal.

He was a very capable and intelligent man, and his only faults were that he was a little too persistent and conservative. For example, the church steeple needed to be repaired. Rather than repair it, he decided to have it torn down and replaced with a cap because this was much cheaper. There were many parishioners who disagreed with this decision because this steeple was one of the tallest and most beautiful in South Eastern Indiana (see the back cover of the book). He persisted and the steeple was torn down and replaced with the stubby replacement we see today. The former aesthetic looks of the church were destroyed. (Figure 3)

Figure 3

On 9/20/1961, Father Ebnet died while sitting in a lawn chair behind the rectory and before the morning mass. He was a large man who was quite tall with a large barrel chest, and it is believed he died of a heart attack. He is buried in the church cemetery next to Father Adam Feigen, the man he was named after at his birth. I am sure that one of the reasons Father Ebnet was so devoted to St. Joseph's had something to do with the fact that Father Feigen also had been a pastor there and was buried in the cemetery. I understand that it was Father Ebnet's request to be buried beside him.

If you visit the cemetery to see this site it will be on the right as you enter the cemetery. Many of the tombstones on the right have German words on them.

The word "Geboren" means "born." The word "Gestorben" means "died."

Father William J. Buhmeier succeeded Father Ebnet as the pastor of the parish. He was a great deal less conservative than Father Ebnet. He also was somewhat tenacious when he wanted something, which many parishioners admired. His tenure was from 8/61 till 7/62. During this short period he brought about many changes. He will always be remembered for two of them.

His major achievement was the expansion of the elementary school. He was able to raise most of the money for the addition to the school, but before it could be completed his health failed and he had to leave. The second initiative he implemented was the removal of many trees that surrounded the church. He had them cut down which changed the looks of the church and the grounds a great deal. Many parishioners were upset over this, and I am sure that upset him a great deal. If he had listened to his parishioners, he might not have had health problems. He eventually died of heart problems in 1986.

His intentions were for the best of the church and we certainly are grateful for the improvements he made to our school. The basement of the school has a kitchen and eating area that can be used by parishioners for social events. Our family has used this area for family gatherings on numerous occasions. This is the location where we gathered to celebrate my doctorate degree from the University of Cincinnati. My thanks to Father Buhmeier!

He was succeeded by Father Lawrence J. Frey. His tenure was from 8/62 till 5/67. His first task was to complete the addition to the school and that was accomplished. The school was completed and blessed on 8/25/1963 (Stenger, 1991). He won the friendship and respect of the parishioners. In talking with them at the time of this writing (1967), they hoped he would be with them many years to come. Unfortunately, that did not happen as he was moved to another parish. It makes you wonder as you look back on the history of the parish: Why is it that the change in leadership is so often? If it were not for Father Ebnet, I wonder where the parish would be today.

I will not describe changes in the church and its population since the 1960's. In 1885, there were 120 families attending the church. In 1910, that number had dropped to 100. Beginning in 1950 that number started to increase, probably as a result of returning WW #2 soldiers. The St. Joseph Church in 2013 is totally different because of the influx of new homeowners. There are subdivisions brought about by the interstate access from Cincinnati. In the days before the influx, you could go to church and everyone would know everyone, if someone was not there, the question would be asked. Why is so and so not in church? Progress! Good or bad! We have to live with it! The St. Leon of 1800's and pre 1960's will never be the same.

The Cholera Epidemic

As a child growing up, I often heard the story of the cholera epidemic of 1848 and 49. Cholera was a national epidemic and thousands were dying on a daily basis. St. Louis, MO reported 670 deaths each day. The parishioners of St. Joseph's decided to pray to St. Joseph and ask him to spare them from the epidemic according to the story. They promised to make March 19th a holy day if St. Joseph would spare them the epidemic. It was miraculous that not a single member of the St. Joseph congregation died from cholera during that epidemic although many in surrounding areas were afflicted with the disease.

The Bells of St. Joseph's Church[1]

The bells were purchased from Vanduzen and Tift Bell Foundry in Cincinnati, OH at a cost of $1046.00. Each bell had a name. The largest bell is five feet in diameter, weighs 980 pounds, has a tone of "A", and is named St. Joseph. The next bell is four feet in diameter, weighs 577 pounds, has a tone of "C", and is named St. Mary. The third bell is three feet in diameter, weighs 342 pounds, has a tone of "E", and is named St. Gabriel. There is a fourth small bell attached to the doorway in the sanctuary. It weighs 196 pounds and has a tone of "A." A list of those 110 parishioners who pledged from $100.00 to $1.00 to purchase the bells can be found in the Stenger history.

Getting the bells up and into the bell tower must have been quite a community event. It is easy to imagine hundreds of people standing around to watch them being pulled in place through use of horses, ropes, and pulleys. The honor of pulling them into place was given to Joe and Mary Bulach. Their horses were used to pull the bells into place. Mary Bulach was also given the honor of being the first person to ring the bells. This honor was a way of saying thank you for housing and feeding the construction workers. There are many descendants of Joe and Mary Bulach still living in the area. My brother Jerry lives on the home place.

Citizens Who Became Priests and Nuns

As you read about the history of this town and its focus on Catholicism and the church, you get the feeling that it was a very religious community. Growing up there, I can attest that it certainly was. Further evidence of this devotion to the church is the number of people who became priests and nuns from this community. There were four men who became priests and eighteen women who became nuns.[1] The four men who became priests or monks are the following:

- Stephen Stenger, O.S.B. He was the son of John C. Stenger, and he was ordained at St. Meinrad in 1880.
- William A. Benz, V.D. He was the son of Frank Benz of South Gate, IN, and he was ordained at the Holy Name Cathedral in Chicago, IL in 1925
- Benno Fellinger, O.S.B. He was the son of George Fellinger, and he was ordained at St. Meinrad in 1942. He was in charge of the Indian Mission at the Queen of Peace Convent at Belcourt, ND.

- Paul Alf O.F.M. He joined the Franciscan Order in 1873 and was ordained into the priesthood in 1877. He died in 1980

There were many more ladies than men who became nuns and they are the following:

Name Taken	Family Name	Date Entered
- Sister Lucy	Magdalene Andres	1897
- Sister Mary Joseph	Anna Andres	1898
- Sister Edeltrudis	Margaret Andres	1898
- Sister M. Leonarda	Josephine Boelsey	1899
- Sister Petronilla	Emma Coile	1918
- Sister Anthony	Mary Doerflein	1929
- Sister Margaret Clare	Hildegard C. Frey*	1915
- Sister M. Laurens	Louise Frey	1902
- Sister Ludgardis	Caroline Frey	1904
- Sister Mary Reginald	Wilhemina Frey*	1921
- Sister Mary Robert	Margaret Gillman	1939
- Sister M. Verena	Mary Hofmeier	1885
- Sister Corsia	Magdalena Moster	?
- Sister Baptista	Josephine Pflum	1898
- Sister M. Bede	Barbara Redelberger	1885
- Sister Inez	Rita Schuman*	1940
- Sister Paulita	Alvira Schuman*	1945
- Sister Mary Verena	Mary M. Schuck*	1897
- Sister Daniels	Elizabeth C. Schuck*	1904
- Sister Bernice	Bernice Stenger	1968
- Sister Magdalena	Agnes Wilhelm	1931

*These are sisters. There may be more, e.g., Andres and Frey, but I do not have the documentation. Further information about these nuns regarding their parents and cousins can be found in the Stenger Parish History.

The Lutheran Church

In trying to describe the population of the greater St. Leon area in the mid to late 1800's, there were also a lot of Protestants in the area. In the 1880's, there were approximately 100 Protestants attending the St.Paul's Evangelical Lutheran Church which is located on the left side of SR 46, just west of the crossroads. This number continued to decline with less than 20 in 1960.

A log church was erected in 1843 and it was replaced with the existing stone church in 1867. [4]It was constructed of limestone which was quarried from the Mason farm near Tanner's Creek. The Masons helped build the church and housed and fed the construction workers. The only remaining descendants (in 1967) of citizens who attended this church are the Amos Beneker family, Alice Beneker Werner and family, and the Ed Oehlman family. Some of the Masons moved to the Guilford/Lawrenceburg area. At the time of this writing in 1967, there was a Joe Mason living in Lawrenceburg who is believed to be a descendant of the original Mason settlers.

There is a good possibility that the Amos Beneker family are descendants of Martin Benninger. He was one of the early settlers who purchased the SE Quarter S11 in 1818. Joyce Baer, the genealogy specialist at the

Dearborn County Library researched this for me and wrote the following: "I searched St. Paul (stone church) Lutheran Church records (1872-1930) and found baptismal, marriage, and burial records for Benekers, but unfortunately records too recent to make a tie into Martin Benninger. We have a newspaper obituary for Martin Beneker (b. 18 July 1917 and baptized at St. Paul) (d.Nov.1972 and buried at Trinity Lutheran Church, Klemmes Corner). Son of John and Emma (Minnemann) Beneker. There is a Henry Frederick Beneker (son of Frederick and Margaret Beckman Beneker—German immigrants) of Highland Twp., Franklin Co. (b. 9 July 1849; d. 10May 1915) who had a son named John. Henry lived and died near South Gate (Franklin Co.), just north of St. Leon. His short one sentence obit (*Register*, May 13, 1915) lists last name as "Benniger" but did not list parents. He is buried at St. Paul's Lutheran Cemetery."

Based on Baer's research and finding a Beneker named Martin and one with Benniger in his obituary, I am confident that Benekers are descendants or related to the earlier Benninger. The last surviving male Beneker was Amos' son Jim, who is deceased. There were a number of female descendants who are still living and they have a number of children living in the greater St. Leon area. I recall that Bill Knue, Joe Stenger, and Leroy Bischoff married Lillian, Rita, and Francis Beneker.

The first pastors of this church were Rev. Misner followed by Rev. Crosshoff in 1867. His successor was Rev. Althoff.[4] No record can be found of the church pastors after Rev. Althoff, and it has not been used by the congregation for many years. At one time in the 50's and early 60's it was rented by a Methodist congregation, but they are no longer there. The church is in a bad state of disrepair and may be beyond repair at this stage.

References

1. Ebnet, A. J. *Unfinished History of St. Joseph's Parish.*
2. History of Dearborn and Ohio Counties, 1885, p. 582.
3. Recorder's Office, Dearborn County Courthouse, Lawrenceburg, IN.
4. History of Dearborn County, 1885, p.593.
5. History of Dearborn County, 1885, p.683-684.
Blanchard, C. (1898). *History of the Catholic Church in Indiana, Volume I,* Logansport, In, A. W. Bowen & Co. *p.68.*
Blanchard, C. (1898). *History of the Catholic Church in Indiana, Volume II,* Logansport, In, A. W. Bowen & Co.
Fette, A. (1951). *History of New Alsace.*
Reinhardt, K. F. (1978) *Germany, 2000 Years* Vol. 1
Stenger, B. (1991). *Throughout the Years in St. Joseph's Parish: 1841-1991.* Archdiocese of Indianapolis: Indianapolis, IN.

Chapter VIII

Military History

The military history began August 24th, 1781during the Revolutionary War. Colonel Archibald Lochry's expedition of one hundred and seven men was traveling on the Ohio River just south of Cincinnati, OH. They were sent to join forces with George Rogers Clark at Fort Vincennes in the war against the Indians who were fighting for the British. They set up camp at a point now called Laughery's Creek where they were ambushed by a band of Indians. There is a historical plaque commemorating this site at the River View Cemetery in Aurora, IN. (Baer, 2013) Sixty soldiers were captured and the rest were killed. The prisoners were taken to Detroit, Michigan and were released after the war.

Two of the men, who were captured and taken prisoner, later purchased land and became citizens of St. Leon. These two men were Valentine Lawrence and his brother-in-law George Mason. More is written about them in the chapter about "Early Settlers." Valentine Lawrence was born in 1758 in Fayette County, PA, and he bought or was granted land in St. Leon in 1817. He lived there until his death in 1827. His burial place is marked by a tombstone*(figure 1) located on the front yard of the rectory and across from the road of the cemetery. It is interesting to note that this was the first cemetery in St. Leon. At one time there were a number of tombstones on this site, but this is the only one left.

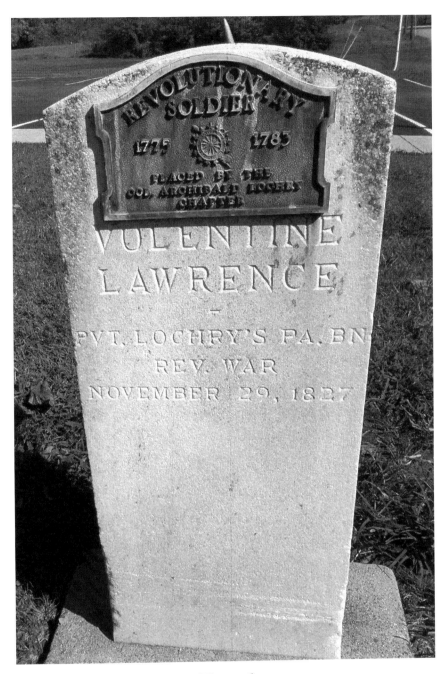

Figure 1

*The spelling on the tombstone using an "O" instead of an "A" is incorrect. All other references to him spell it Valentine.

George Mason bought land along Tanner's Creek in 1819. How long he lived here and where he is buried is unknown. We do know that he was active with the Lutheran church and he is thought to be buried there. Many of the early graves were marked with wooden crosses and those have since disappeared. Many of his descendants are buried there.

War of 1812

The War of 1812 was the next war involving citizens of St. Leon. Those citizens who purchased land here were the following: George Lewis, George Mason, Daniel Mason, Philip Mason, Valentine Lawrence, William Lake, and John Hall. These men were part of General William Henry Harrison's army.[1] They were not directly involved in the war. They volunteered for service and were later ordered back to Indiana to protect the frontier, which is what it was called at that time. They made regular patrols between areas now called Brookville and Aurora. They had several encounters with Indians, but no one was killed.

The Civil War

The next war involving citizens of St. Leon was the Civil War (1861-1865). All told, thirteen citizens fought for the Union during this war. Their names and circumstances are the following: [2]

• Lawrence Hyland	Died from wounds
• Philip Mason	24th Battery Light Artillery
• Frank Mason	24th Battery Light Artillery
• Francis Schuck	52nd Infantry Regiment
• John Andres	Company I 32nd Infantry Regiment (killed)
• John Andres	Entered with 83rd Infantry but could not be accounted for
• George Herbert	Company H 83rd Infantry Regiment
• Philip Gahlert	Company H 83rd Infantry Regiment
• John Gahlert	Company H 83rd Infantry Regiment
• Seth Kelso	Company H 83rd Infantry Regiment
• Joseph Weibert	Company H 83rd Infantry Regiment
• Henry Miller	Company H 83rd Infantry Regiment (killed in the battle at Memphis, TN)
• Benedict Pflum	Company H 83rd Infantry Regiment
• Joseph Bruder	He enlisted in Pennsylvania, and his regiment is unknown

In the various sources and from talking to people from the St. Leon area, I was able to gather some information about some of these soldiers. Probably the most interesting was what I heard about Joseph Bruder. My aunt Marie Pohlman (deceased) told me that Joseph Bruder liked to talk about the Civil War, General Grant, and the day Abraham Lincoln visited him. He claimed to have served under General Grant. He also said that he was in a hospital recuperating from a wound when President Lincoln visited and shook the hands of all the injured soldiers. He did his best to cheer everybody up and improve their morale. He also claimed the distinction of being the only person living in St. Leon to have shaken President Lincoln's hand. He eventually moved to Cedar Grove where he died in 1926. He is buried in the Cedar Grove Cemetery. Irvin and Lester Fuernstein are his great nephews.

The men of the 83rd saw a lot of action. They were involved in the siege and defeat of Vicksburg. They later joined Sherman's army and fought their way through the south in a march destined to go down in history. This was the burn and destroy mission where they destroyed everything in a march from the Mississippi River to the Atlantic Ocean. This included major destruction in Atlanta, GA.

The John Andres referred to above is believed to have joined the 83rd and was lost in action. He was probably picked up by the 32nd, and that is why his name appears on two rosters. He died of his wounds at Murfreesboro, TN in 1863. He is believed to be the John Andres who is part of the family tree compiled by Edward Frey of Cincinnati. Edward married John Andres' niece and she is related to the Andres families that still reside in St. Leon.

Philip Mason was a descendant of the earlier Masons, and he died shortly after being discharged. He is buried in St. Paul's Lutheran Evangelical Cemetery. The

Benekers and Oehlmans are descendants of the Mason family.

Lawrence Hyland was a resident of the area along Dogridge Road. He was part of the Hyland family of school teachers in the area. At the age of sixteen, he ran away from home and joined the Union army. Three months later, he was seriously wounded in a battle with rebel forces and died in an army hospital in Nashville, TN.

A major civil war event in the history of the St. Leon area was Morgan's raid. The main party of these raiders passed through Dover, IN and there is a monument at the crossroads marking this event. Several scouting parties were sent out to look for fresh horses and supplies. One scouting party came over the old St. Leon New Alsace road. This road crossed Tanner's Creek and came toward St. Leon on what is now called Dogridge Road. They bivouacked at the old Hyland School which has since been destroyed. The location is the entrance to the Herzog subdivision where the road makes a sharp dogleg right.

They planned to advance on St. Leon the next day, but the citizens of St. Leon scared them by exploding gun powder on an anvil. The powder was weighted down and when it exploded it made a very loud noise. The men responsible for this action were John Frey, John Stenger, and Charlie Wilhelm. This is the story as told to me by some of the old timers in St. Leon.

Another scouting party camped on the Schuler farm south of Dover. Mary Schuler, who married my great grandfather Joseph Bulach, told this to her son John Bulach. John Bulach was my grandfather, and I heard him tell this story when I was a youngster. According to Mary, the scouting party took all of their animals and grain and left them destitute.

Nothing is known regarding citizens of St. Leon being involved in the Spanish-American War.

During WW I, thirteen citizens took part in that war. Of these thirteen, two are known to have died. They are Albin Leonhard Ratz and Edward Beneker. Albin Ratz was the son of Joseph and Mary Witt Ratz who died shortly after his birth. He was reared by his uncle Nicholas Ratz. In 1917, he drowned off the coast of France. He is buried in a cemetery at St. Nazain, France.[3]

Edward Beneker also left St. Leon and never returned. He disappeared in action, and nothing is known about what happened to him. It is speculated that a bomb killed him and so destroyed his body that he could not be identified. There is a grave stone in St. Paul's Lutheran Evangelical Cemetery as a reminder of his existence.

The remaining eleven men are the following: Joseph Bischoff, Oscar Feller, August Frey (wounded), Frank Glaub, Alois Hoffman, Sr., Joseph Hoffman, Joseph Orschell, Leo Orschell, William Orschell, Harry Stumpf, and William Stumpf.

During WW II, a great many of St. Leon's young men served their country. Four of these young men paid the ultimate sacrifice and were killed in action. These four men are the following: Robert Gillman, Carl Schuck, Paul Schuman, and Melvin Stenger. Melvin and Paul often worked on the farm for my dad. They would often give me piggyback rides and horse around with me. I was very fond of them and was sad to see them leave for the war.

At the end of the war, there was a funeral for all four men, and they were buried in the church cemetery. Their gravestones are the first ones on the left of the road as you enter the cemetery. (Figure 2-5) I vividly remember this ceremony and was emotionally very distraught. The playing of taps and the firing of shots commemorating their service brought tears to many of the citizens that morning.

Figure 2

Figure 3

Figure 4

118

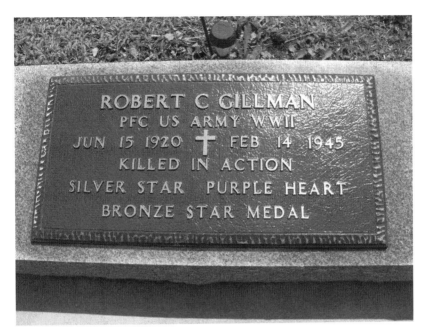

Figure 5

Figure 6

The other young men who served and fought for their country are the following:

- Edgar Andres, Edmund Andres, Paul Andres, Richard Andres, Victor Andres, and Wilbur Andres.
- Alois Bischoff, Earl Bischoff, Elmer Bischoff, and Irvin Bischoff.
- George Eckstein (wounded).
- Cornelius Feller (wounded), George Feller, and Leroy Feller.
- Robert Fox.
- Lawrence Frey.
- Howard Fuernstein (prisoner of war) and Lester Fuernstein.
- Harry Gillman and Francis Gillman.
- Joseph Glaub.
- Albert Kraus, Leo Kraus, and Victor Kraus.
- Julian Ober.
- Albert Schuman (wounded), Leroy Schuman, and William Schuman.
- Earl Stenger, Harold Stenger, Leo Stenger, and Sylvester Stenger.
- William Telker.
- Raymond Trabel.
- Marvin Vogelsang.
- Eugene Weldishofer and William Weldishofer.
- Edward Wilhelm and Richard Wilhelm.
- Ralph Wuestefeld.

While many men served their country during WW II, there were also two young ladies who served. One was my aunt Cornelia Bulach, and the other was Ella F. Andres. Aunt Connie, as we called her, entered the Army Nurses Corp as a 2nd Lieutenant. Ella Andres entered the Women's Army Corp and performed clerical work. Both ladies faithfully served their country for the duration of the war. One can only imagine the courage it took to volunteer for service and leave this small town. Growing up in St. Leon was a very isolated way of life, even when I was a youngster. Imagine what it was like in the 40's to go to war and serve your country. That took courage, guts, and something that is missing in many elements of our society--pride in the good old USA!

There were a number of men from St. Leon who were decorated for valor during WW I & II. Anyone who was wounded received a Purple Heart. Soldiers who qualified for this medal are the following: Edward Beneker and August Frey who served in WW I. WW II recipients were: George Eckstein, Robert Gillman, Cornelius Feller, Carl Schuck, Albert Schuman, Paul Schuman, and Melvin Stenger. Robert Gillman also had a Silver Star. The Silver Star was awarded for gallantry/valor in action. With three medals, he was the most decorated WW II soldier.

The Bronze Star was awarded for heroic service and for action above and beyond the call of duty. Recipients of this medal are the following:
- Joseph Andres, Victor Andres, and Vincent Andres.
- Leroy Bischoff.
- Robert Gillman.

- Andrew Hornbach.
- Edward Oehlman.
- Joseph C. Schuman and Richard Schuman.
- Jerome Stenger and Theodore Stenger.
- Alvin Werner.

The American Legion

Shortly after WW II, the American Legion St. Joseph Post 464 was formed and named after the patron saint of St. Leon. (Figure 6) It was organized in 1946 and the charter was granted in 1947. The building was erected/built in 1957 and since then many additions and renovations have been made. It has been a focal point and has served the many varied needs of the community. It consists of a dance hall, kitchen, large eating area, and bar. It is used for meetings, weddings, family reunions, etc.

Other than providing a comfortable environment for gatherings, dances, and other events, the members of the Legion also contribute to charitable events. They donate money to Knightstown, which is the home for orphans of sailors and soldiers. At Christmas they donate to needy families in the area. They also conduct memorial services on five cemeteries. Two of these cemeteries are at Cedar Grove and the other three are at Blue Creek, St. Leon, and St. Peters.

The Legion Post is a great asset to the community and continues to play an important role today. Were it not for the role of the Ladies Auxiliary, however, it would not be as successful. They fulfill a very important function in the post.

The role of St. Leon citizens in conflicts after WW II has not been researched for this book. A number of citizens did serve, but it was difficult to determine the where, what, and when. For example, I served from January of 1957 to January of 1960. I was a member of the 82nd Airborne Division. I enlisted right after Korea and was discharged before Vietnam. My only action was a military maneuver designed to scare Castro in 1959. During that maneuver, we parachuted into the country of Panama and conducted war games. The Bay of Pigs invasion occurred shortly thereafter, and I was not part of that either. As you can see, I was not part of any military action, but I did serve my country.

References

1. History of Dearborn and Ohio Counties, 1885. P. 201.
2. Grecian, J. *History of the Eighty-Third Regiment. P. 141.*
3. *Indiana Adjutant General's Report.* Vol. VII 1867. P. 774.
4. *Indiana World War Records,* p. 129.
Baer, J. (2013). *St. Leon, Indiana—History.* A power point presentation at the Lawrenceburg, IN Public Library.

Chapter IX

Political History

The political history of St. Leon is best explained with one word "Democrat." The citizens of St. Leon have always been Democrats. With the influx of new residents moving from Cincinnati and elsewhere that has changed, but until the 1960's there were very few Republicans in St. Leon. There is one event each presidential election year that seems to symbolize the enthusiasm the citizens have for the Democratic Party. That event is called the "pole raising."

The Pole Raising

This event dates back to the political rallies held to elect Andrew (Old Hickory) Jackson. In many cities across the US, political rallies were held in support of Andrew Jackson's run for the President of the US. The only city that still recreates the "pole raising" is St. Leon. An article that appeared in the November 3rd, 1960 edition of the Lawrenceburg Register does an excellent job of describing the pole raising tradition in St. Leon.

"A traditional ceremony that dates back to 1828, when Andrew (Old Hickory) Jackson was campaigning for the President, and has been observed at St. Leon each Presidential election in the 132 years since then, was perpetrated Saturday afternoon when a Democratic pole-raising was held there.

It was the most colorful and well-attended event of its kind ever held in this little Kelso Township town. An estimated 2,300 persons were present, representing all parts of Dearborn County as well as other parts in Indiana and Ohio.

In preparation for the event an 85 foot hickory tree, grown in the woods of John Alig, a prominent party worker of that community, who has donated many of the hickory poles for previous events, had been hewn, trimmed, and moved to the school yard by John Alig, Alfred and Leroy Schuman, and Earl Bischoff. These four men were in charge of the arrangements. At the top of the pole, they attached the Democratic emblem—a rooster painted on metal enclosed with a metal frame, made many years ago by Hillman Tebbs and kept especially for these events.

Combining for a festive air at the school yard as the large crowd assembled, were the huge hickory pole supported by wooden braces and ready to be raised into position; a donkey hitched to a cart decorated with bunting and candidate posters, a Ford Roadster, also decorated in red, white, and blue. Perched in the seat was a live crowing rooster. The Brookville and Dearborn County fife and drum corps and other musical ensembles along with photographers and reporters were also part of the festivities.

Led by the donkey cart, the crowd, carrying candidate banners, formed a parade around the square and returned to the school yard. The pole was then hoisted aloft by 60 men who pulled on ropes to place the pole in position and secure it. The American flag was then hoisted above the rooster emblem, and the spectators stood at attention as the strains of the 'Star Spangled Banner' floated out over the air."

I was one of those 2300 people who attended this event on that warm afternoon. I was amazed at the way they raised this hickory pole. The pole was resting on an X shaped bracket which caused the end of the pole to be about six feet off the ground with the butt positioned in the hole. The men grabbed the ropes and one of them gave the command "Pull!" and all pulled on the ropes at the same time and the pole moved several feet up in the air. The command "Pull!" was given again, and again, and again, until the pole was straight up in the air. It was amazing and exciting to see how this was accomplished.

Anyone attending this event in St. Leon today would find it difficult to imagine what it was like when St. Leon was in its heyday. In the late 1800's St. Leon was quite a different town with its stores, distilleries, mills, and other shops. In order to give the readers a look into the past and what it was like in those days, I want to share an article about the pole raising from the October 6th, 1876 edition of the Lawrenceburg Herald.

"The Centennial Guards, in their beautiful and handsome uniforms under command of their officers Captain Louis A. Stemler, First Lieutenant J. Brush and Second Lieutenant Joseph Schue, were taken to the pole-raising at St. Leon last Saturday by the Hudson and Buetman boys, who furnished eight horses each to draw the large hickory wagons, constructed for this use. Gaffga Bros. string band accompanied them. The boys in their uniforms numbering 61 were the center of attraction during the entire day.

At Dover, on their way to the pole-raising, they were halted and treated to the hospitalities of that generous place. At St. Leon, the freedom of this corporation was extended to the boys; and a jolly good time they had of it, for St. Leon is where the unterrified Democracy knows no opposition--not a Republican being in the bounds of the entire city or a single Republican vote being cast in the entire district."

Another article in the same edition describes the participation of some citizens of the neighboring town of Dover and New Alsace in the St. Leon pole-raising.

"Hurrah for St. Leon, Dover, New Alsace, and the bully boys of the Centennial Guards! Dover reciprocated with a fine turnout the assistance furnished from St. Leon at her pole raising. Three hundred of the steadfast and enthusiastic Democrats marched from here to attend the pole raising at St. Leon last Saturday. Old Uncle Jimmy Carpenter says he is ready with his teams and boys every day if he can only advance the glorious cause of Democracy, and Walter Connolly, Milton Kuntz, and Michael O'Conner furnished their horses to draw the big rally wagons and went to the meeting on foot. I mention this to show how unselfish in their adherence to the grand old principles of Democracy are these honest horny-handed, bighearted sons of toil, ever ready to labor and exert themselves to further the ends and progress of honest reform."

These two articles capture the enthusiasm and excitement that was generated by the pole raisings in each community back in the late 1800's. St. Leon is the only town remaining in the United States that still continues with this tradition. Anyone who wants more information on this can go to the internet and type "St. Leon pole raisings."

In the 1876 article, it was written that the "unterrified Democrats of St. Leon know no opposition." That is simply not true! There are stories that I have heard about hickory poles that were cut down. Someone decided that the hickory pole with its flag and rooster at the top had to come down. So the story goes, during the night someone cut the pole down. Was it pranksters or one of the few Republicans in the area? We will never know the answer to that question.

I remember in 1960 that the marshal Earl Bischoff was alerted to be on the lookout for potential vandals who might want to cut it down. Earl lived just across the road from the school yard and could easily keep an eye on the hickory pole. Just as a precaution, I remember seeing people drive a bunch of nails into the base of the pole in case someone wanted to use a saw to cut it down. The nails would make it difficult to saw it down.

The Rooster Becomes a Symbol for the Democratic Party

One other interesting fact about the St. Leon pole raisings is about the rooster as the symbol of the Democratic Party. This appears to be an Indiana thing because the donkey is the national symbol of the Democratic Party. That came about because the supporters of John Quincy Adams, who was running against Jackson, called him a "jackass." Since then, the donkey has been the symbol of the Democratic Party.

The rooster became a symbol of the Democratic Party because of a political campaign for a seat in the lower house of the Indiana State Legislature. Joseph Chapman from Greenfield, IN was an acclaimed orator and was noted for his ability to speak or as they called it "crowing." The campaign slogan was "Crow Chapman Crow!" He won the election and the rooster became the symbol for the Democratic Party. The source for this information is the internet. Just enter Democratic Party and rooster and you will find lots of information on this topic.

Citizens of St. Leon have always been politically active in State politics. John C. Stenger came to the US and started a blacksmith shop in St. Leon and later owned flour and saw mills in town. He was a very successful businessman and was elected to the State legislature in 1865. From 1868-70 he was a Kelso Township trustee and became a county commissioner in 1872 (Baer, 2013). Both he and his brother Joseph, who was also a merchant, played an active role in the political activity of the area. John C. Stenger's home was just east of town on the left. In the 1960's that house was somewhat abandoned. I went in that house and I was amazed at the construction of the entrance and the many other unusual and very attractive features of the house. That property has since been purchased by St. Joseph's Church personnel for future use.

I am not aware of who was politically active since J. C. Stenger, but I do recall Betty Bischoff who was the Dearborn County Auditor from 1971-78. Her brother Robert (Bob) Bischoff was a State Senator from 1977-78 and a State Representative from 1980 to 2010. Joe

Andres was a deputy sheriff for the county for a number of years. Dennis Kraus was the county surveyor for a many years. He was the grandson of Joseph Kraus, who is my mom's father. So I believe we can say that the citizens of St. Leon have been politically active.

Now we get to the interesting question of what is going to happen to politics in St. Leon in the future. It has always been Democratic, but will it continue to be that way? The citizens of St. Leon tend to be conservative and the Democratic Party tends to be liberal. When I moved to Georgia in 1993, the State was solid Democrats. In 2003, Democrats, who were conservative, began defecting to the Republican Party. Today, Georgia has a Republican Governor, State Senate, and House of Representatives. It has gone from a Democratic State to a Republican State.

Will the same happen in Dearborn County and St. Leon? Is it possible that "the unterrified Democracy" will know opposition? Will many conservative Democrats in St. Leon change parties? Will the pole raising continue if most citizens are no longer Democrat? I hope so because it is a great tradition, and it would be a shame to see it abandoned because the citizens of St. Leon change parties. On my recent visit to St. Leon in April 2013, I was told that during the last pole raising in 2012, there was a Republican presence that inhibited the festivities somewhat.

References

Baer, J. (2013). *St. Leon, Indiana—History*. A power point presentation at the Lawrenceburg, IN Public Library.

Chapter X

System of Town Government

All towns need some form of government and St. Leon was no exception. This is especially important because St. Leon is a corporate town. As a corporate town, they could receive money for schools, roads, and other maintenance needs. Were it not for the corporation, these duties would be the responsibility of the county.

No one knows for sure when the corporation was formed. A search through the records at the Lawrenceburg Courthouse also found no information. Father Ebnet spent a great deal of time trying to find out when and why the corporation was formed. He did not find the exact date, but he did discover that it was formed during Father Scheidler's pastorate from 1860-1874.

The reason for the corporation was to receive money from the State to build a school large enough to close some of the one room schoolhouses. There was one east of town and one west of town and possibly the one at Southgate that they wished to consolidate. The new school was built in 1865 and was a concrete two story structure directly across from the front of the church and next to the cemetery. Consequently, the corporation was probably formed before 1865 depending on how long it took to get the money and build the school.

As stated earlier, the main reason for forming the corporation was to create a public school and be eligible for State financial assistance. As I think back on this, most of the students studied catechism and went to church every day. I don't know of another public school where that happened? Maybe I am wrong on this, but I do recall the school superintendent from Lawrenceburg visiting our school on occasion.

It was also rumored that the corporation was formed in order to get the many businesses in town to pay a larger share of the cost of education. In summary, the town formed a corporation for three reasons: 1) to consolidate the one room schoolhouses; 2) to get State financial assistance; and 3) get more financial assistance from the town's many businesses.

In 1967, the governing body was the town board composed of three trustees and a clerk-treasurer. An election was held every four years to re-elect or elect new officers. I believe that is still the current governing structure. The clerk-treasurer is bonded by a bonding company to protect the financial expenditures of the town.

Board members meet once a month to perform duties, make laws, and decisions for the town's safety and operation. For instance, in 1947 they passed a law requiring police protection at all dances held in the town. I am not sure if that law was ever enforced? I attended a lot of dances in the barn Joe Schuman used to store feed and equipment, and I do not recall seeing police protection.

Another law passed in 1948, stated that no automobile could be parked within twenty-five feet of the intersection. That is another law that I do not think was enforced? When I was a kid many cars parked within 10 feet of the corner. There used to be a weighing scale on the right side of the road and in front of the tavern door. It was not unusual to see two or three cars parked in front of it. In 1948 though, there were two gas pumps by the front door of the general store. That may have been the reason for the law. If a car parked there, anyone wanting to buy gasoline would not be able to do that.

They have the additional duty of maintaining all the roads of the corporation. At the time of this writing in 1967, the marshal was responsible for overseeing the condition of the roads. For example, if the trustees decide that a new culvert should be installed, or something removed from a road, it was the marshal's duty to see that this was carried out. Whether this practice is still followed in 2013 is unknown to me?

They have the responsibility of maintaining the budget as well. They receive money from taxes levied on each citizen that is collected by the county. There is money from the corporation tax, gasoline, and liquor taxes. Another source of income is the gambling tax from the riverboat gambling enterprise on the Ohio River at Lawrenceburg and Aurora. This additional source of income has allowed trustees a little more freedom in developing their budget.

Some Decisions of Town Board Meetings (1914-1963)

In order to give the reader of this book some idea of the kinds of decisions that the trustees had to make, I will select some decisions that were made from 1914 to 1963. (taken from the minutes of Town Board Meetings as they were written)
- 5-1914, Board suggested that a concrete bridge be built on the road from South Gate to St. Leon.

- 11-1-1915, Ordered that all tax holders be present to work out road tax. They should be present at the stone pits in person or have a suitable substitute*.
- 12-31-1918, Balanced the books: Total income $1088.00, Total expenses $1013.00 with a balance $75.00.
- 9-1-1919, Increased the town tax from $0.75 to $1.00 of assessed valuation.
- 5-3-1920, Ordered that all heavy hauling be stopped when roads were not fit and gave all town officials authority to enforce this law. (I recall as a kid, that some roads when the spring thaw came had ruts over a foot deep. Getting stuck and ruining a road was probably the reason for this decision.)
- 10-4-1920, Ordered the marshal to get the rock crushed as soon as possible, to get all hands together, to supervise them and not to let one man haul rock or work by himself.
- 10-7-1921, Rented stone crusher to John Andres for $30.00 an hour.
- 8-7-1922, Accepted sealed bids for the purpose of crushing stone, with stone to be crushed by the yard and the bidder furnishing all necessary hands and engine belt.
- 7-6-1925, Paid Pete Andres $30.00 for land for new road leading down Logan Creek.
- 9-3-1925, Frank Geis agreed to build new road for $168.00. (At the time of this writing that roadway was still visible. It was on the north side of the creek and made Cincinnati and Harrison more accessible. There was another road east, but there was a very steep hill to climb just east of the Lobenstein farm.)

*Any citizen who was unable to pay the road tax could work out what they owed.

Some other significant events that involved the trustees are the following:
- 1931, Trucks were used to haul gravel, and the town received the benefit of the gasoline tax.
- 1942, The area in front of the church was blacktopped.
- 1948, The State Highway Commission was requested to post no parking signs and restrict parking of vehicles within 25 feet of the intersection.
- 1954, Dearborn County gave permission to use their road grader once a month.
- 1956, The American Legion was given a road right of way and permission to build their building west of town.
- 1961, Two lights were installed to provide lighting of the street.
- 1963, Resolved that the public road running parallel with Logan creek and beginning at S.R. #1 be closed to traffic and cease to exist as a public road. (U.S. #46 made this road obsolete.

In the early days, road upkeep was a never ending task and every taxpayer paid their fair share of the cost. In the early days, the mud roads as they were called were gradually covered with crushed rock. Later with invention of trucks and the development of roads, gravel replaced crushed rock. As a teenager, I remember only one mud road in the corporation. It was a road between Richard and Pat (McCann) Schuman's house and Chuck Andres' house and across US #46 from Walter

Schuman's farm. That road is now closed. Most roads today are blacktopped making road upkeep less of a problem. Today's trustees deal with a whole new set of problems with the influx of subdivisions and the increase of citizens moving into the St. Leon area. They created a Planning and Zoning Board to oversee this process.

Chapter XI

Important Events/Happenings

In this chapter, I will describe how the citizens celebrated certain events during certain seasons of the year, New Years, St. Joseph's Day, Christmas, Fourth of July, the Pole Raising, etc., and compare them to how that may have changed.

New Year's Eve

A logical starting point is the first or end of the year and that is called New Year's Eve. Around 1900, that was celebrated in an entirely different way than it is currently celebrated. In those days, a group of young men would band together and visit various houses in the town around the midnight hour. This is the story as it was told to me by my father. This group of young men all had shotguns and probably had a few drinks earlier that evening. They were usually a very loud and boisterous group, and some were a little drunk. The group had a leader and the leader, on arriving at a house, gave a "Spruch." (This is the German word for a "Speech."

The speech told the people living in the house that the group wanted food and drink, and if they did not get it, they would bring in the New Year with a bang. To make sure the owners got the message, each member of the group discharged their shotguns into the air. If this did not succeed in getting the owners out of bed to give them food and drink, they tossed fire crackers up near the bedroom window.

There were a few occasions where even that did not get the owners to come down and serve this rabble rousing group. So the group went to the next step in their plan to get some food and drink. Each member of the group placed the butt of their shotgun against the outside wall of the house. The leader gave the signal to fire and the simultaneous blast and recoil created a tremendous noise. The recoil against the side of the house was strong enough to shake the house and crack the plaster on the inside wall. I was told this last step was only used once or twice. Once the word got around about what would happen, the owners got out of bed and provided food and drink. The group would meet with the owners and celebrate the New Year in good spirits. The group would move on to the next house a little more boisterous and loud into the wee hours of the morning.

Such was New Year's Eve at the turn of the century. An advantage of celebrating this way was the impossibility of having a wreck on the way home, no matter how intoxicated a person was. Keep in mind that there were two distilleries in St. Leon and every farmer had two to three 50 gallon barrels of wine and cider in the basement. There was no shortage of alcoholic beverages in those days. The real danger was that somebody might get a load of buckshot from one of the shotguns. I was told by my father that he knew of no instance where this happened.

The invention of the automobile changed the way New Year's Eve was celebrated. Typically, some organization held a dance in Schuman's barn or at the

New Alsace church hall. A favorite when I was a teenager was Coonhunter's Lodge in Batesville. Many families celebrated by having a party in their own home and invited neighbors and relatives.

Some of the men would engage in activities to show their physical prowess. My dad loved to get a broom stick and show how agile he was. He would hold the broomstick in both hands and put one leg through, and then he would bring it up behind his back and get his other leg through without losing his grip on the broomstick. Depending on how much the other men had to drink, there were only a few who could repeat it.

Prior to the 1950's, all entertainment was created by those attending the party. Playing cards was a favorite and there was always someone at the party who could play an instrument. My dad could play the harmonica, and I remember George Feller (Yatz we called him) could play the accordion. As a kid, I remember some of these parties. It seemed like everyone really enjoyed themselves. How they celebrated changed with the invention of television, home movies, DVD's, stereos, etc. Today's New Year's Eve parties have so many more options on what they can choose for entertainment.

St. Joseph's Day

The next event of importance was St. Joseph's Day on March 19th. This day was a holy day for those who attended mass at St. Joseph's Church. As mentioned earlier, everybody in St. Leon was Catholic except for the Oehlman and Beneker families. In the 1800's this meant going to church, no work, and a visit with friends and relatives. It is no longer celebrated in this fashion and probably changed somewhere around the 1950's. Many residents worked in factories or had jobs in Hamilton, Cincinnati, Lawrenceburg, or Batesville and had to go to work.

The practice of celebrating St. Joseph's Day began in 1848. It was in this year that the dreaded cholera plague was killing thousands of people in surrounding communities. The citizens of St. Leon met in the old log church and prayed to St. Joseph to spare them from the plague. They vowed that if St. Joseph could find a way to protect them any deaths, they would always keep his day holy. It was somewhat of a miracle that no one from St. Leon died from the plague, while deaths in surrounding communities continued. As a token of their gratitude, the citizens proclaimed this day a holy day. It is still a holy day in St. Leon, but it is no longer celebrated as it once was in the 1800's and early 1900's.

Easter

Another highlight, following soon after St. Joseph's Day, was Easter. A common practice was an old German custom to hide eggs in the grass during the week prior to Easter Sunday. My mom told me that the Easter Bunny was practicing so things would not go wrong on Easter Sunday. Every day we would go outside and look to see if there were any eggs to be found. Sometimes mom hid them in strange places, like the woodshed. We were so excited to go out and look for these eggs.

These eggs were different than the ones we got on Easter Sunday. Every one of these eggs was colored brown while those on Easter Sunday would all be different colors. Mom would save the outside peelings of the onions from the garden. These would be the brown dried up outside peeling of an onion. She would save these and use them to color eggs. If you put a bunch of these peelings in a pot of water and boil them with eggs, they turn a beautiful brown color. I am not aware that anyone still follows this custom, but it sure was fun for us.

Another custom/practice associated with Easter was the eating of candy. In our family, we stopped eating candy on Ash Wednesday and the beginning of lent. So for 40 days we ate no candy, but on the Saturday before Easter, we were allowed to eat candy at noon. While we could not eat candy, we could save it. So we all had baskets where we stored our candy. I remember that I kept mine in the attic and would often go there and just look at it. By the time noon came on the Saturday before Easter, we usually had a pretty good basket of candy.

The Summer Kitchen

Summer was not far behind, and the next event of importance was moving all kitchen equipment to the summer kitchen. Back in those days, all farm families had summer kitchens. My brother Jerry still uses the summer kitchen as a sort of a hangout. He and his son Jeff had remodeled and it is a place for friends to hang out and have a few drinks, play cards, etc. (Figure 1).

Figure 1

The practice of moving all kitchen equipment to a summer kitchen was necessary prior to the invention of air conditioning. Summers were hot and there was always a lot of cooking and canning. A well-ventilated area was needed. The summer kitchen had windows on all four sides and usually two doors with screens. This allowed for good air circulation. There was also the cleaning required because of work in the fields. This kept all the dirt in one room and made cleaning after farmers and field hands a lot easier. When fall came all kitchen equipment was moved back to the main house. Most farm households discontinued this practice once air conditioning became available.

Seen on the left side of the summer kitchen is the smokehouse. This was used to smoke and preserve meats. Prior to refrigeration every farmer had a smokehouse. This is another aspect of early American living that is no longer practiced.

Burning the Fields

There was another practice in those days that has been discontinued. It was the practice of burning off a field. Many farmers burned their fields to control pests and weeds. Sometimes those fires got out of control and required that every able body grab a shovel and a wet burlap sack to beat out the fire. Growing up I recall two or three of those fires that got out of control. One was across the road from our house on the Wilhelm farm. Another was back on Dogridge Road close to Tanner's Creek. Bill Freeman was cleaning out a fence row and the brush he was burning got out of hand. I witnessed that fire and it required about 10 local farmers to beat it out.

The Fourth of July and Dance Floors

The 4th of July was the next big event for the citizens of St. Leon. A typical affair was an old fashioned house party. The largest room in the house would be cleared and used for a dance. It has been said that the Joe and Mary Bulach had many a party in their brick home on the hill west of St. Leon. The house was built by the Newman's and one room was large enough for affairs of this sort. The house was torn down in 1927 because the bricks were soft and deteriorating. A new wooden structure was built to replace it, and that structure is the home of Jerry and Carolyn Bulach.

Another common practice in the 1800's was having a picnic in somebody's woods where a dance floor had been laid for the occasion. The dance floor was constructed in the woods because this was the coolest place to have one. Everyone was invited to come and take part in the festivities. They would play games like horseshoes and cards, dance, and gossip with their neighbors. There would be lots of wine, cider, and other beverages to drink and lots of food. It was a very festive event.

The practice of laying dance floors in the woods was changed in the early 1900's. By this time dance halls had been built for festivities of this type. There was one in New Alsace that I played in as a child. It was across the road from the Albert Kraus home. It was a big barn with a large dance floor and benches around the outer walls. Dances were no longer held there in the 1950's. It was just used as a barn, and that barn has been torn down.

There was another one at Zimmer's Grove on old US #1 going toward Dover. It probably would have been close to the Zimmer farm which is now a golf course on Hyland Road. Joe Schuck had a dance hall at Highland Center, and there was also one at Lawrenceville. Joe Schuman built a barn that was used to store feed and equipment. It was also used as a dance hall. It even had a raised stage where the band could play. I went to many dances in that barn. It would be cleared of feed and equipment and the floor was excellent for dancing. There was many a square dance in that barn. In the 1950's, American Legions were constructed in most towns by the returning WW #II soldiers. All of the Legion Posts had large dance floors and there was no need for other dance halls.

Figure 2

The Potato Derby

The last of these early dance halls to be used was the one in St. Leon built by Joe Schuman. There was an annual competition called the Potato Derby to see who could grow the largest potato. There was a fee to enter the competition and the potatoes would be planted in the spring and harvested in the fall. Each entry would have their largest potato weighed, and the person with the largest potato would be the winner. The weight of a large potato was usually in the two to three pound range with some going a little larger. The last function of the competition was a dance and chicken fry to be held in the Schuman barn. (See Figure 2) The winners of the contest would be honored and given their prizes. I recall that my brothers Wes and Jerry won this competition a few times. I remember attending some of those dances in the 1970's. Interest in this competition waned around the year 2000. In a recent conversation with folks in St. Leon, they are trying to restart this competition.

The Church Picnic and Harvest

Shortly after the harvesting season and starting in the 1920's there was the annual church picnic. It was a way to raise money for the St. Joseph Parish. It was a lot of work for the members of the parish. There were potatoes to peel, chickens to be plucked, cakes and pies to bake, etc. There were stands and tables to assemble. It was a great time for the community to come together and have a good time despite all the work involved. This all changed in the 1940's when Father Ebnet suggested that donations replace the church picnic. Many of the parishes in nearby communities still continue with their church picnics. They are well attended, the food is excellent, and everyone has a good time.

In the fall, nut hunting, squirrel hunting, picking apples and making cider were events that brought people together. It was important, at that time, to store nuts to be cracked over the winter for cooking and eating. Squirrels represented fresh meat which was very important because refrigeration had not yet been invented. Apples were important for a number of reasons. They could be stored in the cellar and eaten for a long period of time during the winter. My mom would peel them and cut them into slices and they would be placed on the tin roof of the smoke house to dry. Once dry, they would be placed in a cloth sack and hung in the attic. I often sneaked into the attic and took a handful of these dried apples. They were an excellent snack. Of course I was not supposed to eat these apples because mom wanted them for cooking.

Nowadays, nuts, apples, and meat are purchased at grocery stores. The old practice of drying apples, cracking nuts, and making cider are infrequent events. I remember many hours spent sitting on the stone steps by the granary with my hammer and cracking hickory and walnuts for mom to use in baking pies and cakes. Saturdays were the days that baking for the week was done. If dad did not need me for outside chores, I got to help mom. I always enjoyed that a lot more than cleaning manure out of the chicken house. Mom had a routine that was the same every week. Saturdays were for baking and taking baths, Mondays were for the laundry, and on Fridays, mom always had bean soup and she made something we called "good stuff." It was scrambled eggs with a little tomato juice instead of milk and some bread crumbs.

Halloween

Halloween was a big event back then and still is today. Back in the 1800's and early 1900's there was more tricking than treating. Few families had candy or other treats to give, so there was a lot of tricking. I remember one morning after Halloween seeing a buggy/carriage on the roof of the department store across the street from the tavern at the crossroads in St. Leon. Sawing down trees to block a road also occurred. Turning over outhouses and corn shocks was a favorite trick as well. Back in those days, if you got caught, there was a reprimand and restitution. Today, law enforcement will put you in jail, and this has reduced this practice of tricking.

Hunting and Trapping

Winter meant hunting and trapping. Trap lines were set and muskrats, coons, skunks, mink, rabbits, and opossums were trapped. Some were trapped for meat and some were trapped for furs. Mink furs brought a very good price and even skunk furs were profitable. For example, a skunk fur brought from 3-10 dollars depending on the markings. I remember that I set up my first trap line when I was about 12 years old. I had about 12 traps set at various holes on our farm. The best holes were those in sink holes, and some were groundhog holes. I would get up around 4:30 to run my traps so I could be back home around 6:00 to do the milking.

I want you to stop and think about this for a minute. Imagine how this is so different from what might happen today. Here I was, a very young kid, running trap lines in the winter all by myself. My dad said I had to run those trap lines every day because if an animal was in a trap I had to release it or kill it. There were days when the ground was covered with snow and the temperature was below zero. I ran those trap lines seven days a week with my dog, flashlight, and rifle. What parent today would allow their kid to do something like that?

In the 1800's and early to mid-1900's rabbit hunting was very important because it was a way to get fresh meat to eat. I remember that Thanksgiving Day was always one that was spent rabbit hunting. My brother Wes, dad, and sometimes one or more of our uncles would head out with our beagle to hunt rabbits. We would form a line and head across a field or meadow. It would not be unusual for us to kill a dozen or more rabbits in a day. My dad had an eagle eye and he could spot a rabbit sitting in the bushes better than anybody else. It was uncanny. He would say, "there sits one!" I would look and could not see it. He would take his 22caliber pistol and shoot it in the head.

Some hunters around the turn of the century trained ferrets to go into holes, catch a rabbit and bring it out to their owners. This was especially valuable in the winter when snow was on the ground. You could see the rabbit tracks go into the hole and you knew the rabbit was in there.

There was a demand for rabbit meat amongst the citizens of Cincinnati. At that time, John Schuman had a huckster route and he would buy rabbits and sell them to people in Cincinnati. I was told that he paid $.025 for a rabbit and sold several hundred a week. This practice was discontinued when refrigeration was invented. Eating rabbits was still a major food source even in the 1950's. I used to raise tame rabbits and sell them for a dollar. I usually raised 50 at a time and always sold all of them to people from Cincinnati who visited our farm and bought eggs and other farm items.

Christmas Preparation and Christmas Eve

When I was a kid, December 6th was always a special day. On this day Santa came and got our Christmas wish list. We would put it on the box for firewood and it would mysteriously disappear. This is a German tradition, and it takes place in honor of St. Nicholas. This is the day devoted to this saint, and he is responsible for Santa Claus. In addition to giving Santa our wish list, one other thing happened.

The guest bedroom would be locked the next day, and we would be told that Santa was in there getting things ready for Christmas. We were told to be good or we would not get anything for Christmas. I remember trying to look under the crack of the door to see what I could see. I also tried to look in the windows, but they were covered. It was a mystery. We knew Santa was in there, but we never heard any noise from that room.

On Christmas Eve, Santa would come, and he would ask us if we had been good. He usually carried a switch which he kept hitting against his boot. We were often scared to death that he was going to hit us with it if we did not give the right answers to his questions. None of us, however, ever got switched. When he was through questioning us, he would take a key and open the door to the guest room which had been locked since December 6th. To our amazement, there would be this decorated Christmas tree and presents. We did not get many presents in those days, just one or two. One present we always enjoyed was fruit and nuts which Santa always brought. It was not often that we got fruit and nuts, except for hickory and walnuts.

Christmas Eve ended with midnight mass at St. Joseph's Church. Everyone in town was present for this special occasion. There would often be visiting priests and bishops. It was a very festive occasion with lots of Christmas carols and singing. With the shortage of priests today, there are no visiting priests or bishops, and many families today celebrate Christmas on Christmas day.

In the 1800's, Santa Claus also had a wife who accompanied him for Christmas. She was called Chris Kindle, which is a German word for Christ Child. She was always dressed in a white robe. Santa also had another name. He was sometimes called Belschnickel. I have no idea regarding the meaning or origin of this name. I just remember hearing people say "I hear Belschnickel coming!"

Back in those days, Santa Claus always came to your house to distribute the presents. In some cases there was more than one Santa Claus. The typical routine would be for Santa to take his switch and hit several windows on the house to get our attention. We would go excitedly from window to window until he knocked on the door. Dad would go out to meet with him and offer him a drink. Santa would come in and question us, open the door to the guest room, give us our presents and depart to visit the next five or six homes to distribute presents and talk to excited children. Sometimes, after the five or six drinks that were consumed, Santa became very jolly.

Looking back on the good old days, with the corn husking, threshing machines, dance floors laid in woods, Halloween shenanigans, and Christmas traditions, much has changed. There was a need for people to come together to get things done. With all the modern inventions there is a lot less interaction between people. The need for ten or more farmers to plant or harvest a crop has been replaced by one farmer with modern equipment. In the late 1800's and early 1900's, everybody in St. Leon worked on a farm except for those who had one of the businesses in St. Leon. Some of those business owners also had a farm, as for example my great grandfather Joseph Bulach, who owned the general store and tavern in St. Leon and the farm currently owned by my brother Jerry Bulach.

Organizations of St. LeonThat Bring People Together

There are three organizations in St. Leon that still bring the citizens together for fellowship and to get things done. Those three are the Conservation Club, the fire department, and the American Legion. All three organizations have many citizens who are very active and provide functions that are enjoyed by all. The Legion has a large hall, basement, and outdoor facilities that can be used for weddings, reunions, and dances. More information about this organization can be found in the chapter on military history.

Figure 3

The conservation club has a nice facility east of St. Leon. (Figure 3) Its location is in a wooded setting about a half mile off the road. It is used for meetings and turkey shoots. They focus on conserving wildlife and providing a place where members can sort of hang out and have a good time. In earlier years when I was a kid, the members met in Schuman's barn. We sat around on feed sacks during the meeting and after the meeting there was a fish fry and beer. The fish were whiting and I can still remember how good they tasted.

Plans for the fire department were begun on March 13th in 1967. In April of 1967, a fire truck and pumper were bought for 1400 dollars. The building for housing the equipment was completed in 1969. (Figure 4) It is a volunteer fire department and owes its existence to the diligence and hard work of the citizens of St. Leon and to its first officers. The president of the newly formed department was Andrew Hornbach and the vice president was Walter Schuman. The fire chief was Ted Stenger, and the secretary treasurer was Albert Schuman.

Figure 4

The fire department has an annual festival that draws people from as far away as Cincinnati. Members are very active in keeping the building and equipment in good repair. Response to the need to put out a fire is very quick, and they are very effective in putting out fires.

One fire that was described to me did not involve the fire department. It occurred in 1889 and Father Ebnet related the story to me. He stated that Barbara Ruff told him that the fire occurred around noon just after Sunday mass. She said that it was so intense that it threatened to burn down the whole town. Somehow Andrew Aug's barn which was located about 1000 yards south of town mysteriously caught on fire. It was very windy that day and sparks from the fire were flying everywhere. People had to get up on their roofs to put out the sparks for fear their roof would catch on fire. Father Seibertz, who was pastor at the time, asked a local painter by the name of Dan Ruff to go up on the church roof and pour water on the wooden shingles. [1]

There are several versions regarding how the fire started. One version is that the Aug boys were shooting pigeons and sparks from their guns or friction from the bullet set it on fire. Another version is that the Augs had a bull tied in the barn and some mischievous boys wondered how high the bull would jump if a fire were built under him. Regardless of how it started, there was a very big fire in St. Leon that almost burned down the town. With the modern equipment of the St. Leon fire department, that danger no longer exists.

The Fox Hunt

An event that occurred once or twice a year was the fox hunt. I took part in one of those hunts when I was about 10 years old. My mom, older brother, and about 100 other people from Dover, New Alsace, and St. Peters also took part in the event. The hunt took place on the south side of US #46 and east of US #1 on a Sunday afternoon in the fall of the year. Sometimes we had one in the spring. In talking to other people, fox hunts took place in other communities as well. They were always on a Sunday afternoon.

The setup for a fox hunt was quite ingenuous. It required a lot of people and a lot of noise makers. There were two sets of people: the noise makers and the shooters. The noise makers lined up about 5-6 feet apart along US #1 and formed a line about a quarter mile long depending on how many people showed up. The shooters would number 10-15 people, and they lined up about a half mile away below the hill on US # 46 towards Harrison, OH.

The process would start with a lot of camaradie, a few drinks, and some snacks. Then the lines would form. The line with all the noise makers would ring cowbells, bang on pots, and in general make a lot of noise as they advanced toward the shooters. The noise would frighten any foxes or other game toward the shooters as the line advanced. As the line came closer to the shooters, each end would move in toward the shooters forming a large arc in the shape of the letter "C." The shooters would shoot all the foxes they saw and any other game they wanted. Most game was let through so the noise of the guns going off did not scare the foxes. Everyone had a lot of fun, and it was a very enjoyable outdoor experience. As far as I know, the shooters never injured any of the noise makers.

The Tavern, Bull Gang, and Nicknames

As mentioned earlier, the tavern was a gathering place for the farmers to gather and get paid for any produce that was sold. This occurred every Monday night when Joe Schuman gave them their money for the produce he had sold that day on his huckster route to Cincinnati. Naturally, some of the farmers had a little too much to drink and some funny things would happen. One story involved two farmers we will name Ed. Both farmers had recently bought a new pickup truck and both were the same color, make, and model.

The first Ed left the tavern and got in the wrong pickup truck and drove it home. The 2nd Ed got in the other and drove it home. Neither one knew that the truck was not theirs. So the story goes, it was about a month later that one of the realized an object on the key ring that was not his. The first Ed went back to the tavern and asked the bartender, who else in town had a blue pickup truck. The bartender told him that he knew a guy who came to town now and then, and his name was Ed. The two met and swapped trucks according to the story.

Growing up in St. Leon, there was not a lot to do for amusement so we had to get creative. We formed a gang called the "Bull Gang!" We decided that was a good name because everybody was afraid of bulls. I remember many dreams where a bull was chasing me, and I would come to the fence and could not get over it. At that point I usually woke up in a cold sweat. Jim and Denny Callahan, Raymond and Stanley Wilhelm, and my brother Wes and I made up the gang. Sometimes Wilfred Bischoff joined our gang.

Riding our bikes back to Virgil Werner's store and buying a pint of ice cream, buying a bottle of RC Cola and putting a pack of peanuts in it were two of our favorite activities. Getting into mischief was always on our minds. Having fun with one of the farmers leaving the tavern who had a little too much to drink was another of our forms of mischief. Our favorite was to put a block of wood under one of the rear wheels of their car so it was off the ground about a half inch. They would get in their car and put it in gear and the car would go nowhere. I recall one time when one farmer went through all the gears and just sat there for over 15 minutes before he realized that he was going nowhere.

The farmer would go back into the store to get help when he realized what was wrong. As soon as he left, we boys who were hiding over the wall in the church yard would get up and remove the block. When the farmer got back with his helpers to remove the block and found the car okay, he would get teased that he had just had too much to drink.

The funniest of these escapades involved my dad who had been given the nickname "Shorty." It seems that everyone in town had a nickname. I recall such names as Bounce, Pussyfoot, Squirrely, Lefty, etc. Why or how that practice began I am not sure. My nickname at one time was Smiley.

The incident with my dad involved another farmer named "Shorty," and we had put a block of wood under the left rear tire of his car. He came out of the tavern and got in the car, started it, and put it in gear. He raced the engine so loud that we popped our heads up to see what in the world he was trying to do? He saw us, recognized my brother and me, and knew what we had done.

He got out of the car and went back in the tavern to tell my father. My brother and I went to the open window outside the tavern to see what was going to happen. The farmer went to my father and in German said: "Shorty! Hast du zwei Buben? Einer so hoch und einer so hoch? Translation: Do you have two boys? One this high and one this high?" Each question was accompanied by hand movements of height.

My dad responded with "Ja!" At that point the other Shorty switched to English and said: "Well those two sob's have jacked up my car. The entire tavern of farmers erupted in laughter. My dad did not even mention it to us when he came home. I've tried to describe what it was like to grow up in St. Leon, and what it was like in the mid-1800's and early 1900's. Some of it is very personal, and I hope that did not detract from the more historical aspects of this history.

The last paragraph of the 1967 version of this history expressed my wishes. At that time, I wrote the following:

"I wish that I could have written more about St. Leon, and I apologize if I have an incorrect detail or missed something or someone of importance. My other wish is that the reader enjoys reading about St. Leon as much as I enjoyed digging through old books and papers and talking with the elderly residents of St. Leon, while gathering information for this history. In parting my third wish is best expressed with an old German phrase which I heard quite often as a child growing up in St. Leon.

That phrase is 'Mach's gut!' Translated that means 'make it good' or the equivalent of 'Have a good one!'"

References

Stenger, B. (1991). *Throughout the Years in St. Joseph's Parish: 1841-1991.* Archdiocese of Indianapolis: Indianapolis, IN.

About the Author

Dr. Cletus R. Bulach attended the two room schoolhouse at St. Joseph's for grades 1-8 (1944-1952). He attended Guilford High School for his freshman and sophomore years and transferred to Sunman High School for his last two years and graduated in 1956. On graduation he began work at the Sperry Rubber factory between Cedar Grove and Brookville.

In 1957, he joined the army and qualified to become a member of the 82nd Airborne Division. He served three years as a ballistic meteorologist and made 20 jumps. After discharge, he again was employed by Sperry Rubber as a guard during the strike. At that time he also enrolled as a full time student at the University of Cincinnati. He graduated in 1964 with a bachelor's degree as a teacher of German and History.

His first teaching assignment was at Western Hills High School in Cincinnati in 1964. He received his Master's Degree in 1969 from Xavier University and his doctorate in Educational Leadership from the University of Cincinnati in 1974. During his career, he was a teacher, assistant principal, assistant superintendent and a superintendent in three different school districts. After 30 years, he retired in 1990 and sought employment as a college professor.

He was an associate professor at Murray State University (1990-1993) and at the University of West Georgia (1993-2003). He retired and was awarded associate professor emeritus status at the university. He is the author of numerous articles in educational journals and is co-author of the book *Creating a Culture for A High*

Performing School: A Comprehensive Approach to School Reform, Dropout Prevention, and Bullying Behavior. The reform and school culture described in the book create a learning environment where students' five basic needs are met. This leads to improved test scores and a 75% reduction in student discipline and misbehavior problems. His website is www.westga.edu/~cbulach. There are many publications on his website describing his research about school culture and climate, bullying behavior, leadership behavior, human relations, and character development.

Anyone wishing copies of The History of St. Leon should send him an e-mail (cbulach@comcast.net) or a letter to 7256 Confederate Lane, Villa Rica, GA 30180

Soft cover copies are $20.00 and hard cover are $25.00.

Made in the USA
Columbia, SC
14 October 2024

43548034R00096